AFRAID GOD WORKS,

AFRAID HE DOESN'T

AFRAID GOD WORKS,
AFRAID HE DOESN'T

TERRY RUSH

The purpose of Howard Publishing is threefold:

*Inspiring holiness in the lives of believers,

*Instilling hope in the hearts of struggling people everywhere,

*Instructing believers toward a deeper faith in Jesus Christ,

Because he's coming again.

Howard Publishers
3117 North 7th Street, West Monroe, LA 71291-2227

Printed in the United States of America

Second Printing 1993

ISBN# 1-878990-15-2

Contents

Foreword

God's people have two options—faith or fear.

We can follow the invisible God into impossible dreams. Or we can cower to earthly fears and follow into predictable routines.

We can see with the eyes of Joshua and Caleb, or we can squint with the cataracts of the timid. We can sing with Paul and Silas or complain like the faithless. We can praise God in the lion's den like Daniel. Or we can throw dreamers in the prison like Herod.

We can walk in faith or fear.

Terry Rush, in the book you are holding, masterfully depicts our choices. Let me urge you to read this book. Allow yourself to be challenged to soar on the wings of courage. Permit your heart to be touched by a supernatural God. Beckon God to scatter the fear and stir the faith in your heart.

Read this book and join with me in thanking God for granting Terry such a timely message.

Max Lucado

Acknowledgments

I am indebted to a mighty crew who, one by one, shared their insight and effort toward this book. Kyla Keesee put in extra hours at the typewriter. Steve Smith and Steve Stalcup made their office facilities and assistance available at a crucial point in the work.

Rachel McArtor decoded my scribbles and transferred them onto the word processor. Linda Jones advised me in regard to grammatical direction. Alton Howard, Gary Myers, and Philis Boultinghouse of Howard Publishing have been a tremendous support. Philis took the rough draft and made it smooth.

A hearty round of applause I give these friends. This was heavy labor. Each one was there for me.

Too, a special thanks goes to three terrific men; my shepherds. Bob Gardner, Jerry Ishmael, and Harriel Scarsdale have given me the room to grow and the freedom to develop.

Kyla, Steve and Steve, Rachel and Linda, Alton, Gary, and Philis, Bob, Jerry, and Harriel. . . .
. . . I love you and I thank you.

Terry Rush

Introduction

The church has moments when it is in the groove. As a well-oiled machine, it clicks away with enjoyable productivity. But at times the church has fallen into a rut. The groove has been worn deep . . . so deep we have reached an impasse. God is always willing to lead us farther. But the rut has us hemmed.

Musical chairs has gradually eliminated kingdom factors. Faith and work were the survivors, and the music was on with only one chair left. Being the heavier, work has rudely bumped faith onto the floor. Work is heavily seated as winner.

Faith was crowded out by confidence in works. Soon after, fate was credited rather than faith. Coincidence emerged to be more reliable than believing in God. It should be no surprise that fear has unmercifully yanked the rug out from under the Christian.

Twenty-five percent of Americans claim to be Christian. Dallas Willard asks if a quarter-pound of salt is enough to cure a pound of meat, why is Christianity not potent? We have cashed in our faith in the activity of legions of angels for the work of a few good men. We have traded grace for grit.

Faith ever wishes to be restored. As we dabble in it here and there, insecurity brushes against our hearts. We want to do, be, and see faith properly. We want God to work but are afraid He will. He might do more than our leadership could control. He might sweep through our system and change out all the bulbs. It scares some to consider just some of what He possibly might do.

The flip side of the coin is that we want Him to work, and we are afraid He won't. We desperately need His affirmative action; yet fear squelches the hope.

God works. He works with us . . . in us . . . and even for us. May this book offer faith. May fear take a brutal beating. May you develop a taste for faith.

Do not pray for easy lives; pray to be stronger people! Do not pray for tasks equal to your powers; pray for power equal to your tasks.
Phillips Brooks

Terry Rush
747 S. Memorial
Tulsa, OK 74112

Chapter 1

Rheumatism Has Settled Into Our Faith

Where is our Christ, who is alive and lives in power? In the preaching of our churches, he has become a beautiful ideal. He has been turned into a myth, embodying a theological concept. The witness to his objective reality has largely been lost. Most liberal protestant churches have never even heard of the prayer of power in his name. The church has become an organization of well-meaning idealists, working for Christ, but far from his presence and power.

—Flora Wuellner

Faith is the first and last great puzzle to be attempted. It seems that all the king's horses and all the king's men have, likewise, met the ultimate challenge when it comes to putting the properties of faith back together again. This God-given power has courted our minds with potent influence. But just as the sun slowly sets, we have let this treasure of wealth fade from our hearts into distant regions.

1

Deep persuasions of endearing faith have been dismantled from our hearts over the years. As the waves continually and relentlessly tap, tap, tap at the shore, sore experiences have washed our belief system out to sea. Swept clean on the inside of any positive conviction, have we, perhaps, left our house unoccupied? If we have, surely Fear and his gang have moved in. This has been the most tragic takeover in history. Society is missing something. Faith's absence is causing tremendous strain. Faith in the unknown has been replaced by fear of the unknown. You and I are being hurt by this pollution. It must be corrected if mankind is to survive.

Dallas Willard aptly put it, "What is missing in our deformed condition? From a biblical perspective, that it is the appropriate relation to the spiritual Kingdom of God that is the missing 'nutrient' in the human system. Without it, our life is left mutilated, stunted, weakened, and deformed in various stages of disintegration and corruption."[1]

What is missing? Faith.

Faith, which allows the fullness of God (Eph. 3:16–19) to stir life, has been bartered. Saving faith in God has been exchanged for mental assent to doctrine. Trusting Jesus has been converted into campfire devotionals and support groups. And, the Holy Spirit has been traded for positive-thinking rallies and a Nolan Ryan rookie bubble gum card.

Faith is not necessarily sensible. Neither must it obey the law of rationality. It will buck when saddled by binding logic and reason. With what degree of intelligence and reason did his neighbor credit Noah for building an ark? How bright could Abraham have appeared to the well disciplined as he headed out on a mission not knowing where he was going? (Heb. 11:8).

Yet, he is the father of . . . faith.

Recovery is forthcoming. Words of revival are being whispered. Spiritual paralysis is being curbed, and the fever of fear is beginning to break.

"Have you ever noticed the 'wondering-ness' (if I may coin a word) of the people who go on with God?" asks Oswald Chambers. "They never seem to be overanxious or overconcerned, and they always seem to be getting younger. What is the characteristic of the people of this world who have not got the child-heart? They are always sighing; they have mental and spiritual rheumatism and neuralgia, moral twists and perversities, and nothing can rouse them. Why? They need the child-spirit, the Spirit that was given to the disciples after the resurrection and in its fullness at Pentecost; then nothing will turn them aside."[2]

The basis of faith is the invisible sphere. It is the "conviction of things not seen." Noticing the unseen. Certain of the unseen. Believing there is activity in another realm (an unexplainable realm) is faith.

Faith knows (conviction) a creational God, a resurrected Jesus, a functional Spirit. The mind may acknowledge their existence, but to actually believe that each is a working, moving, unseen part of one's life is faith.

You don't mean blind faith? There is no such

thing as sight faith. Second Corinthians 5:7 calls one specifically to walk by faith, not by sight. When we can see how our plans will work according to our church strategy, we are not necessarily moving faithfully. We may be simply practicing good management . . . from the human viewpoint, that is.

Examples of biblical blind faith are numerous. Abraham believed God could do what He promised when there was no hope for him and Sarah to have a child. His conviction about God's ability delivered a blessing to mankind (Rom. 4:16–21). Esther, Elijah, Moses, and Paul experienced things that baffle the human heart because they were able to see God when they could have withered in frustration and fear.

Unsighted faith can be deeply threatening, because it is spiritual, not fleshly. The next chapter will deal with man's chronic desire to manipulate and control everything . . . including God.

For now, blind faith may sound a sour chord, because it does not fellowship common sense. Sight is not just that physical ability to distinguish between red and green or to know how far it is from here to the curb. It is the mind-set that weighs, considers, and initiates direction the way we normally think . . . a sense that is common to all . . . common sense. Does creation make sense? To faith it does. To many brainy scientists/evolutionists it doesn't. Does the flood make sense? To faith it does. To the philosophy of the world it doesn't. Does the virgin birth fit logic. Never. But faith says, "yes." Does a resurrected Son of God fit into rational consideration? Mankind says "no," while fundamental faith heralds, "Hallelujah!"

See to it that no one takes you captive through philosophy and empty deception, according to the tradition of men, according to the elementary principles of the world, rather than according to Christ (Col. 2:8).

Apparently, God reversed the role that thinking was to play in the new kingdom. Announced as a king, Jesus got off to a shabby start. (Common sense wouldn't begin with birth in a barn.) As a man, he did not receive tidy endorsements from the local entrepreneurs.

Thinking? Yes. But from a different plane. Thinking based on the invisible reality rather than obvious street truth. Reasoning? Yes. A sneak-peak behind the invisible curtains reveals angels at work (Heb. 1:14). The unseen is more than the seen. Blind faith? There is no "sight" faith. Walk by faith, not by sight.

Until we insist that the system of believing is beyond academics, we will be a stifled people. Acknowledging the unseen while forcing these unseen elements to operate by the seen standards is a true disaster. Confusion and, eventually, emptiness result. Is not religion packed with accumulated activity while void of satisfaction and contentment?

We need to be cautious about considering these concepts of faith as "non-sense." The nature of God's approach will appear silly to the fleshly minded.

Where is the wise man? Where is the scribe? Where is the debater of this age? Has not God

*made foolish the wisdom of the world? For
since in the wisdom of God the world through
its wisdom did not come to know God, God
was well-pleased through the foolishness of
the message preached to save those who believe.*

*For indeed Jews ask for signs, and Greeks
search for wisdom; but we preach Christ crucified, to the Jews a stumbling block, and to
the Gentiles foolishness, but to those who are
called, both Jews and Greeks, Christ the power
of God and the wisdom of God* (1 Cor. 1:20–
24).

Where is the logician, the philosopher, the great
preservers of truth? Have they not been discarded
because His approach is so beyond their knowledge, theory, and conclusions? "For My thoughts
are not your thoughts, neither are your ways My
ways, declares the Lord. For as the heavens are
higher than the earth, so are My ways higher than
your ways, and My thoughts than your thoughts"
(Isa. 55: 8,9).

His ways are invisible. Ours lean toward the
seen. The "seeing-is-believing" format is a con.
That which is a stumbling block and foolishness
to both the Jews and Greeks turns out to be the
very power of God.

"The natural man does not accept the things
of the Spirit of God; for they are foolishness to
him, and he cannot understand them, because they
are spiritually appraised" (1 Cor. 2:14). The natural man goes by what he can see. The spiritual
is invisible . . . it is spirit. We must move out of
our thinking and into His. Following our natural

instincts is a mistake. Observation from the higher plane must now be considered.

Oswald Chambers said it well when he penned the following:

> Our Lord did not rebuke His disciples for making mistakes, but for not having faith. The two little things that astonished Him were "little faith" and "great faith." Faith is not what Jesus Christ can do, but in Himself, and anything He can do is less than Himself.
>
> Suppose that God is the God we know Him to be when we are nearest to Him — what an impertinence worry is! Think of the unspeakable marvel of the remaining hours of this day, and think how easily we can shut God right out of His universe by the logic of our own heads, by a trick of our nerves, by remembering the way we have limited Him in the past — banish Him right out, and let the old drudging, worry and care come in, until we are a disgrace to the name of Jesus. But let the attitude be a continual "going out" in dependence on God and the life will have an ineffable charm, which is a satisfaction to Jesus Christ.
>
> We have to learn how to "go out" of everything, out of convictions, out of creeds, out of experiences, out of everything, until so far as our faith is concerned, there is nothing between us and God.[3]

The invisible Holy Spirit gives strength to the invisible inner man to allow Jesus to indwell (invisibly) through faith (not sight) (Eph. 3:16, 17). This intangible component triggers the action of God. How do we know? Because it triggered Jesus.

The centurion emphatically believed that Jesus could heal his servant. Jesus' response? "Truly, I say to you, I have not found such great faith with anyone in Israel. . . . Go your way; let it be done to you as you have believed" (Matt. 8:10, 13).

In Matthew 10:5 he sent the twelve with specific instructions to go only to the lost sheep of Israel. A Canaanite woman came pleading for His mercy that He might heal her demon-possessed daughter. He did not answer her. Why? He knew the approach.

His disciples understood the plot, too. They kept asking Him to send her away. But something happened that reversed everything. It reversed the instructions, the plans, the agreement among the disciples. What happened? Faith entered.

> *But he answered and said, "I was sent only to the lost sheep of the house of Israel." But she came and began to bow down before Him, saying, "Lord, help me!"*
>
> *And He answered and said, "It is not good to take the children's bread and throw it to the dogs."*
>
> (Good point!)
>
> *But she said, "Yes, Lord, but even the dogs feed on the crumbs which fall from their master's table."*
>
> (Better point!)
>
> *Then Jesus answered and said to her, "O,*

*woman, your faith is great; be it done for you
as you wish." And her daughter was healed
at once* (Matt. 15:24–28).

He shifted. Why? Her faith was great! Not her
stewardship. Not her obedience. Not her list of
character references. One thing . . . faith. If we
have seen Jesus, we have seen God. If Jesus responds to the conviction of the invisible, He does
so to show us how God reacts and responds to
us.

Obviously, God loves for us to use faith. It is
impossible to please Him otherwise (Heb. 11:6).
It will be noted with greater detail later that the
problem God had with the children of Israel as
they wandered in the wilderness was that they
had no faith. He called their disbelief sin.

Those wanderers had questions. They had answers. They had opinions and ideas. But they absolutely refused to operate beyond the belief that
what they saw was a greater threat than what
they could not see.

Faith is neither a slogan nor a mere doctrine.
It is the nerve to our walk. We are to step out
with the conviction of things not seen. What is
faith? It is the capacity to see how things could
work out, come about, or develop—completely orchestrated by invisible beings.

Chapter 2

Why Is It So Difficult to Believe?

Something happened in the garden that sent a negative rippling effect down through each generation. And though it is due to sin, it still hits us with a, shall we say, blind spot? From this the church will recover.

When Adam and Eve ate of the fruit, a phenomenal paradox took place. Their eyes were opened, causing them to see a segment of reality they had been blind to. Simultaneously, they went blind to a portion of reality they had previously seen.

As soon as they ate, "Then the eyes of both of them were opened, and they knew they were naked" (Gen. 3:7). Before the sin, had they seen with their eyes? Of course. They saw the tree and its fruit. They possessed an ability to see that was different from sight today. They could see, yet not notice certain things such as nakedness.

When they sinned, their eyesight was impaired by being opened to see more. At the same time, they apparently lost the ability to see what is now the invisible world. As we lose the use of one sense, say hearing, our other senses increase. This seems to have happened to Adam and Eve's sight, shifting from invisible to visible.

One thing clearly took place. As soon as Adam and Eve possessed this alternate view, an entirely foreign sensation emerged. Fear. And to this day it has plagued our efforts to walk with the Creator.

"And he said, 'I heard the sound of Thee in the garden, and I was afraid because I was naked; so I hid myself'" (Gen. 3:10).

We have hidden ever since . . . all because we are afraid. Why are intelligent nations hiding in drugs and alcohol? For fun? No, because they are afraid! Why do committees quench a nerve of faith? Always one reason: fear. Let's hear it—"We are afraid of what it will lead to." Leadership doesn't get this disposition from God, doctrine, or duty. We get it because we are cowards. And, our cowardice was planted in the first garden.

Why does He keep saying, "Why do you fear, you of little faith?" Because faith sees with clear conviction and fear can't see anything but obstacles. Blindness to the unseen activity leaves us mistaken and terribly disoriented. The Israelites said Goliath was so big they couldn't hit him. David said he was so big he couldn't miss him.

Why were the Pharisees offended at the word Jesus spoke in Matthew 15:11? One reason is fear. So He said, "Let them alone; they are blind guides of the blind. And if a blind man guides a blind man, both will fall into a pit." Blindness to the invisible certainties has always been an abrasive interference to walking with and for God.

*Now when the attendant of the man of God
had risen early and gone out, behold, an army
with horses and chariots was circling the city.
And his servant said to him, "Alas, my master!
What shall we do?" So he answered, "Do not
fear, for those who are with us are more than
those who are with them."*

A man of God saw and feared. With "garden
eyes" it is not at all unusual to be afraid because
of what we see. Faith, however, is the conviction
of things unseen (Heb. 11:1).

"Then Elisha prayed and said, 'O Lord, I pray,
open his eyes that he may see'" (2 Kings 6:15–
17).

They were opened. That's how the servant's confusion started. He saw the enemy. Yes, but he
literally wasn't seeing the entire picture. God
opens our eyes to peer into the extra life. "I pray
that the eyes of your heart may be enlightened,
so that you may know what is the hope of this
calling, what are the riches of the glory of His
inheritance in the saints, and what is the surpassing greatness of His power toward us who believe"
(Eph. 1:18,19).

When these special eyes are focused, our perspective changes completely: First, fear is replaced
by hope. Next, the intimidation of uncertainty is
replaced with a vision of the riches of His glory.
Then, when fear is removed by our new vision,
we can see the great unseen power of God working
in earthen vessels.

The parable of the talents reveals a scenario

of three slaves given an opportunity to increase their possessions. The five and the two talents were each doubled. The one? It stayed the one. Those possessing increase were accredited with a special acknowledgment . . . faithful. The one who failed was admittedly nonproductive because he was . . . afraid.

Faith or fear. Belief or cynicism. Fruitfulness or caution. The equation seems to be consistent. The committee willing to risk . . . let go . . . will see their efforts grow. And, as Matthew 25:21,23 states of the slaves, there will be a joy about them. But those who cower will lose what little they had by playing it safe. We do not remain constant. We either increase or decrease upon the basis of faith or fear.

Fear tries to freeze the present. Satisfied with the moment, it proposes strong efforts to preserve the status quo. Faith appraises the hope of the future because it is able to praise unseen Jehovah for the present. The physical, fleshly ability to evaluate will nearly always allow intimidation to interfere.

Observe Paul's carefully worded statement as he addressed the potential of discouragement for any follower of Jesus. "Therefore we do not lose heart, but though our outer man is decaying, yet our inner man is being renewed day by day" (2 Cor. 4:16). Note that the outer fleshly man operated on how he saw the situation from the natural viewpoint.

Continuing the apostle's comment, "For momentary, light affliction is producing for us an eternal

weight of glory far beyond all comparison, while
we look not at the things which are seen; for the
things which are seen are temporal, but the things
which are not seen are eternal" (2 Cor. 4: 17,18).

While we "look not"? Correct. What we see is
merely temporary. Encouragement, motivation,
and confidence are issued when we look at "the
things which are not seen."

A weighty event illustrates this simple truth.

> *And when the disciples saw Him walking
> on the sea, they were frightened, saying, "It
> is a ghost!" And they cried out for fear. But
> immediately Jesus spoke to them, saying,
> "Take courage, it is I, do not be afraid." And
> Peter answered Him and said, "Lord, if
> it is You, command me to come to you on the
> water."*
>
> *And he said, "Come!" And Peter got out of
> the boat, and walked on the water and came
> toward Jesus. But seeing the wind, he became
> afraid, and beginning to sink, he cried out,
> saying, "Lord, save me!" And immediately Je-
> sus stretched out His hand and took hold of
> him, and said to him, "O you of little faith,
> why did you doubt?" (Matt. 14:26–31).*

Amazing.
Simply amazing.
As soon as they saw, they were afraid. When
Peter shifted to the use of faith, he walked. He
did it. And next? But seeing . . . he stopped . . .
and went down.

Anytime one takes fleshly, sighted inventory of any circumstance, trouble is on the horizon. Notice these facts:

- Faith leads to an impossible walk.
- Seeing leads to fear.
- Fear leads to sinking.
- Sinking leads to crying.

"O you of little faith, why did you doubt?" Why *did* Peter doubt? Had Jesus left? Peter simply lost his concentration. He began to "look" at reasons why this would not work. It is uncanny that his shift in viewpoint stopped him from continuing what he was already doing.

The statement that Albert Nolan makes is enforcing. "If a man speaks with sufficient conviction, 'with no hesitation in his heart, but believing that what he says will happen, it will be done for him' (Mark 11:23). And if you pray with the very real conviction that 'you have it already, it will be yours' (Mark 11:24). But if you once doubt or hesitate, nothing will happen."[4]

Peter had proven that man could do what could not be done. But then complications set in. He began to second-guess his move. He could see wind and that seemed to be enough. What's the big deal about wind? Had he not seen the water moments earlier? Water will usually be excuse enough for many a man to curb a brisk walk!

Apparently he hadn't considered the water. He considered Jesus. Why did he later, then, consider the wind? He moved his eyes.

Finally, one last setting will expose hard evidence as to why God wants us to believe, to look at the unseen.

> *"Send out for yourself men so that they may spy out the land of Canaan, which I am going to give to the sons of Israel.". . .*
>
> *When they returned from spying out the land at the end of forty days, they proceeded to come to Moses and Aaron and to all the congregation of the sons of Israel in the wilderness of Paran, at Kadesh; and they brought back word to them and to all the congregation and showed them the fruit of the land.*
>
> *'Thus they told him, and said, "We went into the land where you sent us; and it certainly does flow with milk and honey, and this is its fruit. Nevertheless, the people who live in the land are strong, and the cities are fortified and very large; and moreover, we saw the descendants of Anak there.*
>
> *"Amalek is living in the land of the Negev and the Hittites and the Jebusites and the Amorites are living in the hill country, and the Canaanites are living by the sea and by the side of Jordan." Then Caleb quieted the people before Moses, and said, "We should by all means go up and take possession of it, for we shall surely overcome it."*
>
> *But the men who had gone up with him said, "We are not able to go up against the people, for they are too strong for us." So they gave out to the sons of Israel a bad report of the land which they had spied out, saying,*

"The land through which we have gone, in spying it out, is a land that devours its inhabitants; and all the people whom we saw in it are men of great size.

"There also we saw the Nephilim (the sons of Anak are part of the Nephilim); and we became like grasshoppers in our own sight, and so we were in their sight" (Num. 13:2, 25–33).

(Notice that the very nature of spying anything is to look it over with your eyes.)

Faith said, "We can do it!" Fear said, "Over my dead body!" So? Faith entered forty years later over fear's dead body.

What a battle of seen over unseen.

What did the spies see? The giants. What could they not see? The promise. Their testimony was based on physical sight. "We became like grasshoppers in our own sight, and so we were in their sight."

Nolan, again, responds with, "The world is full of miracles for those who have eyes to see them. If we are no longer able to wonder and marvel except when the so-called laws of nature are broken, then we must be in a sorry state."[5]

These poor men even used the eyesight of the enemy to prove their own cowardice stance. Because of what they saw, they made a statement that seemed wise to them. "The land . . . is a land that devours its inhabitants." And then they wandered for forty years in a land that finally devoured every last one of them.

Why does one need faith? Because we cannot

trust the seen. Seeing is not believing. Seeing is seeing. Unseeing is believing. Walk by faith not by sight.

> *Then he said to Thomas, "Reach here your finger, and see My hands; and reach here your hand, and put it into My side; and be not unbelieving, but believing." Thomas answered and said to Him, "My Lord and my God!" Jesus said to him, "Because you have seen Me, have you believed? Blessed are they who did not see, and yet believed"* (John 20:27–29).

Blessed are we when we do not see and yet believe.

A small girl stands at her bedroom window. The lower floor is filled with nightmarish flames. Smoke rolls in giant strides throughout the framework. From the lawn beneath her window her Daddy insists, "Jump Baby!" "But Daddy, I can't see you for all the smoke. Where are you?"

"It's okay, Darlin'. Jump! I can see you."

Faith is our jump because God can see. We trust His view over ours. We jump by faith—without argument. God sees higher, better, farther, and deeper.

I like the way Willard worded it, "The cautious faith that never saws off the limb on which it is sitting, never learns that unattached limbs may find strange, unaccountable ways of not falling."[6]

The threat to faith must be assassinated. Fear is not to be fellowshipped. Masses are dying because fearful Christians won't overcome personal threat and speak up and out for the Lamb of God. Churches are dying because their own leaders are frightened. Afraid of trouble that appears gigantic (even as the sons of Anak), shepherds hide in meeting rooms. Their discussions involve great labor to avoid trouble. This faintheartedness is driving the spikes back into His hands.

Faith in Jesus will lead us to trouble. Jesus insists on it (Matt. 10:34). No man has ever been more controversial than the hallowed Son of God. Many warnings have been given about the distaste God has for the fearful. Yet we bathe in fear. Certainly not all the leaders do. More certainly, enough do to warrant this discussion.

Faith rebels against the norm. Let it be emphatically stated that faith does not upset the apple cart. Fear does. Faith rebels only against the upset. Altizer said, "Genuine Christianity is the ultimate form of rebellion."[7]

Disturbance to any life is not because of faith, but rather the lack of it. We keep looking for help, looking for answers. Looking. Ever watching. Those eyes, again. The solution is in the way we see . . . how we see . . . what we see.

Oswald Chambers wrote, "Are we mourning before God because we have not had an audible response? Mary Magdalene was weeping at the sepulchre. What was she asking for? The dead body of Jesus. Of whom did she ask it? Of Jesus, Himself, and she did not know Him! Did Jesus give her what she asked for? He gave her something infinitely grander than she had ever conceived—a risen, living impossible-to-die Lord."[8]

So it is. Able to look for the dreaded, let us be challenged to seek the working of God. As was for Mary, the answer is in front of our noses because God has done His homework. He calls us to see Him at work. Fear grips us like the suction of quicksand. Faith releases us to mount up like eagles and soar to newer and higher levels of life. Dare to disarm the threat to faith. Rebel against it. Use your eyes by looking beyond the obvious into the region of the invisible.

Chapter 3

Does God Work Today?

Do I believe that God engineers my circumstances, that it is He who brings me each day into contact with the people I meet? Am I faithful enough to Him to know that all I meet with every day is absolutely under his dominance and rule? Do I face humiliation with a perfect knowledge that God is working out His own will?

—Oswald Chambers

If God doesn't work today there is no need for faith.

God works.

There is a need for faith.

Scandalous efforts are made to strip away the motivational approach of a Christian . . . simple faith. False teaching and false believing have reduced it from the walk of a disciple to a word used in Christian literature—and especially within church buildings.

It means nothing.

Aggressive, daring faith has been milked and

drained. Worldly-wise men, under the guise of
church leadership, seldom call wonders faith. They
choose to reduce these wonders to a more manage-
able concept. We begin to hear "coincidence" or "it
just worked out that way." Even the phrase "the
providence of God" is used to soften the truth of
His activity.

For this reason, churches are dying and members are drying up. Little life remains in such an
approach. Assemblies gather and assemblies dis-
miss . . . empty.

Empty. Dry. Dead. But still faithful to the truth?
No way.

Faith is not a word. It is a life-giving pattern
by which we are to walk. It breathes. Faith knows,
senses, expects, anticipates, and drives followers
of Jesus to impossible dimensions.

Faith insists that God is working.

False faith insists He doesn't.

I sought God in prayer to help me restore a
man, whom I hardly knew, to his walk with God.
Not knowing how to contact this person, I prayed
persistently. Out of the blue, he called my office,
explained a spiritual dilemma and asked if I could
come to his house to help. As a result he recommit-
ted his devotion to Christ.

Did God do that? Yes. If He didn't, why pray?
Why bother? Why not sit on our hands and let
the world fall-where-it-may? Let me be emphatic.
This is precisely what many do. They don't pray—
not because they don't believe in prayer—far, far
worse—because they don't believe God works.

Does God work today? Yes. Does God work today? No. Which is it? God responds to the sensor of faith. He does not work for those who believe He does not work.

Another way. If you believe He does not work, He does not . . . for you. One crotchety, stubborn, preacher pleaded, "In the name of reason, God doesn't work that way." He had it right. God doesn't work in the name of reason. He works because followers believe in the name of Jesus.

The fuse is blown, and faith is tripped in a doctrinal blunder that has left the body of Christ disfigured. Wherever there is unusual emphasis on works, there is decline in faith. This leaves a person unknowingly stranded in the very position he thought he had left. Sadly, he's stranded in the center of his own life—dependent on his own, terribly weak energy.

When self-surrender leads one back to self-responsibility for works in the kingdom, hope fades and hearts fold. Look at the countless neighbors who gave up—not on us—but on themselves. They couldn't provide for themselves, nor be their own god. They could not work enough to save themselves.

A Christian is to work. But the work is not going to match the thinking of fleshly-sighted, business-kind-of-thinking people. Our real work is to believe.

"They said therefore to Him, 'What shall we do, that we may work the works of God?' Jesus answered and said to them, 'This is the work of

God, that you believe in Him whom He has sent.' "

What's the question? What kind of work does God want? What's Jesus' answer? Believe.

Do works please God? Yes, if it is the effort He asked of us. "And without works it is impossible to please Him, for he who comes to God must be involved and believe that God rewards hard work." This is how we may practice it. But this is not what the word really says. (It is not uncanny that many reading this think it was quoted properly.)

"And without faith it is impossible to please Him, for he who comes to God must believe that He is, and that He is a rewarder of those who seek Him" (Heb. 11:6).

Believing is work (John 6:29). It is harder work to believe in the invisible than it is to work desperately in the physical. It takes greater grit to trust than it does to lead or follow. The wide road is filled with workers in chain-gang form. It is the narrow road where the faithful traveler is found.

Anyone can work hard—even without God. But you can't believe God will be there unless you work His way. Trust the unseen.

We live in fear and work as hard as we can. So many are afraid God works and afraid He doesn't.

We do see the needs in our local and global communities. We do feel the pressure. We do experience the pangs of compassion. We do hear the call of God to deliver the endangered. But, as we will see later, Martha-ites aren't the answer. Jesus is.

Martha-ites can't take the time to pray, to be

still and know He is God. How can they be still when there is so much work to be done and so few to do it? Did Jesus take action? Of course. He worked on his relationship with the Father before he did anything else.

A promise is given that an invisible code known as the Holy Spirit would provide power within each . . . worker. The sin is not in the doing. The sin is that we are doing with virtually no time spent on hearing God.

Religious activists hate this kind of talk. They don't know God. All they have available to justify their religion is self-effort. This kind of person is obsessed with work. They teach, but are seldom found in a class to be taught. Why? To them there is nothing to learn. They must work.

They must be noticed. They must convey that tired look. They must always be on the scene . . . first. Why? They are staying ahead of the rest of us on the progress charts. They may be grouchy and irritable and snappy and egotistical. But at least they are busy little beavers doing so much good.

Hardly.

Such only pleases ourselves and a few of our cronies. Our faith is in our works when our work ought to be in our faith.

Should we teach? Should we help? Should we care? Should we give? Should we pray? Should we reach? Should we serve? Should we lead? Should we listen?

Didn't Jesus?

He did all this and more, because He believed

the Father. He did not do these things because
they were the trademark of a good and faithful
man. Listen to Him in regard to Martha-ism.

> *Now as they were traveling along, He entered
> a certain village; and a woman named Martha
> welcomed Him into her home. And she had a
> sister called Mary, who moreover was listening
> to the Lord's work, seated at His feet. But Mar-
> tha was distracted with all her preparation;
> and she came up to Him, and said, "Lord,
> do You not care that my sister has left me to
> do all the serving alone? Then tell her to help
> me."*
>
> *But the Lord answered and said to her,
> "Martha, Martha, you are worried and both-
> ered about so many things; but only a few
> things are necessary, really only one, for Mary
> has chosen the good part, which shall not be
> taken away from her"* (Luke 10:38–42).

(I'm guessing Mary caught it from Martha after
Jesus left.)

Don't miss the point. Doing good and working
in the church isn't the problem. Making works
your religion instead of faith your work is. Believe
God can accomplish the impossible, the mysteries,
the invisible. Don't believe God is thrilled because
you salved your own conscience by being busy.

"For I bear them witness that they have a zeal
for God, but not in accordance with knowledge.
For not knowing about God's righteousness, and
seeking to establish their own, they did not subject

themselves to the righteousness of God" (Rom. 10:2,3).

Not aware of the works of God that make one right with Him, these people had drive and enthusiasm and established their own criteria. Even today, we find satisfaction in our own deeds rather than waiting for God to move.

"He saved us, not on the basis of deeds which we have done in righteousness, but according to His mercy, by the washing of regeneration and renewing by the Holy Spirit" (Titus 3:5). The visible? Man's deeds. The unseen? God's mercy. Our work? Believe in God's mercy. This is our deed.

Noah exemplified working faith. Note the wording carefully. "By faith Noah, being warned by God about the things not yet seen, in reverence prepared an ark for the salvation of his household, by which he condemned the world, and became an heir of righteousness which is according to faith" (Heb. 11:7).

"Get with it." "Get with the program." "Keep it moving." "Let us work." "There's so much work to do and so few to do it."

We hear so much of this jabber that Bible words "rest," "wait," and "easy" sound like four-letter words. We are so paranoid that someone might discover that we actually rest, that if we should be awakened to answer the phone at 2:30 A.M. and the caller asks, "Were you asleep?" we'd deny it.

Unclarified and unfocused works have made our religion a lie.

If we are going to reach 500 or 5000 new people,

something has to change. We are trying to land on a runway without any landing gear. By calling on the dimension of His Presence, the approach to increase will be smoother. If we do not shift gears, we will crash in our approach.

In reference to church growth, I believe we are leading our people to rely on involvement to keep people in the church. Once again, we yield to the image of work. Keep working, keep busy, get them involved and hopefully they'll hang in there. This faulty reasoning seems to be verified when relatively new members leave for greener pastures because they didn't feel needed. They didn't have a job to do.

So we get busy developing jobs. We become church employment offices. Believing what? Believing that if we can get this couple active they'll stay around. It usually "works."

What would happen if we remodeled this kind of sheep-keeping tendency? Have we not, somewhere along the way, traded in our relationship with Him for a work order? Do we no longer feel compelled to know Him as much as we feel driven to do a sacrificial deed?

> *You have been severed from Christ, you who are seeking to be justified by law; you have fallen from grace. For we through the Spirit by faith, are waiting for the hope of righteousness. For in Christ Jesus neither circumcision nor uncircumcision means anything, but faith working through love. You were running well; who hindered you from obeying the truth* (Gal. 5:4–7)?

Somewhere, someone led us away from grace, away from faith, and away from truth. We have minimized, if not significantly lost, any posture of a relationship with God. We have defaulted on fellowship with the invisible Father, Son, and Spirit.

Where do we read: go baptize, get them involved, and they'll not go out the back door? He says that knowing the Father and the Son is eternal life (John 17:3).

Does a Christian ever do anything? Yes. The doing is not only essential but is profoundly fruitful when our effort is given to relationship (John 5:19; 15:4,5). We must get our people involved. The commitment, though, is to emphasize attachment to the invisible glory of God, rather than the visible glory of fleshly accomplishment.

As new Christians are added, what if their life revolved, not around a physical church, but around a spiritual kingdom? Would they have anything to do? Immediately. They would have a lot of praising to do to the Father. They would have a lot of praying to do for each neighbor—for a specific nation. They would have a word from God to read, to meditate upon. They would have a God to thank, a God to praise, a God to beseech. Hours worth!

There is so much believing to be done.

The opposition will be quick to point out the fallacy of this thinking by assuring us that this approach would definitely leave us with a teacher shortage, preacher shortage, and, worst of all, a worker shortage. Oh, I don't think so. We already have that now.

I became aware of the possibility of changing

our church growth tactic when I studied Acts 2:41–
47. Three thousand souls were added. Between
that event and verse 47, where God added to their
number daily, what works did they do? How did
they go about giving those new converts jobs so
they wouldn't go out the back door?

They didn't work by superficial deed-earning
standards. They built relationships with one another and with Him. Out of this time when faith
was incubated, gracious, effective workers evolved.

Here's the point: We are putting our people to
work to keep them faithful, when we ought to be
developing their faith to keep them working.

Until we convert our church-growing strategy,
I can see us able to add tens and hundreds. Maybe
there will even be a church or two with eighteen
hundred or twenty-six hundred. Even if we could
find five with five thousand (which we can't), we
must see that we are doing something that is keep-
ing us slow and small.

Does God work today? Certainly. Let us put His
part/our part into precise perspective. When our
goal is to receive the reward of wonderful life,
even after the grave, our work is to believe God's
promises regarding eternity. Who will raise the
dead, transform the bodies, clothe the bodies, give
instructions regarding the new habitat, and pri-
marily provide salvation? God? You?

God.

Does God work today? He better.

"Lord, Thou wilt establish peace for us, since
Thou hast also performed for us all our works"
(Isa. 26:12).

Chapter 4

The Word Declares His Present Activity

For what the Law could not do, weak as it was through the flesh, GOD DID; sending His own Son in the likeness of sinful flesh as an offering for sin, He condemned sin in the flesh, in order that the requirement of the Law might be fulfilled in us, who do not walk according to the flesh, but according to the Spirit.

Romans 8:3,4

For consider your calling, brethren, that there were not many wise according to the flesh, not many mighty, not many noble; but God has chosen the foolish things of the world to shame the wise, and God has chosen the weak things of the world to shame the things which are strong, and the base things of the world and the despised, God has chosen, the things that are not, that He might nullify the things that are, THAT NO MAN SHOULD BOAST BEFORE GOD. But BY HIS DOING you are in Christ Jesus. . . .

1 Corinthians 1:26–30

*Create in me a clean heart, O God, and renew
a steadfast spirit within me.*

Psalms 51:10.

*But let all who take refuge in Thee be glad,
let them ever sing for joy; and MAYEST THOU
SHELTER THEM. . . .*

Psalms 5:11

*Now to HIM WHO IS ABLE TO KEEP you
from stumbling, and to MAKE YOU STAND
in the presence of His glory blameless with
great joy. . . .*

Jude 24

*Jesus therefore answered and was saying
to them, "Truly, truly, I say to you, the Son
can do nothing of Himself, unless it is something HE SEES THE FATHER DOING; for
whatever the FATHER DOES, these things
the Son also does in like manner.*

John 5:19

*So then it does not depend on the man who
wills or the man who runs, BUT ON GOD
WHO HAS MERCY.*

Romans 9:16

*For thou, O Lord, hast made me glad BY
WHAT THOU HAST DONE, I will sing for
joy AT THE WORKS of Thy hands.*

Psalms 92:4

Now to HIM WHO IS ABLE TO DO EX-CEEDINGLY abundantly beyond all that we ask or think according to the power that works within us, to HIM BE THE GLORY in the church and in Christ Jesus to all generations forever and ever. Amen.

Ephesians 3:20,21

And my message and my preaching were not in persuasive words of wisdom, but in demonstration of the Spirit and of power, THAT YOUR FAITH SHOULD NOT REST ON THE WISDOM OF MEN, but on the POWER OF GOD.

1 Corinthians 2:4,5

What then shall we say that Abraham, our forefather according to the flesh, has found? For if Abraham was justified by works, he has something to boast about; but not before God. For what does the Scripture say? "And Abraham believed in God, and it was reckoned to him as righteousness."

Now to the one who works, his wage is not reckoned as favor, but as what is due. But to the ONE WHO DOES NOT WORK, BUT BE-LIEVES IN HIM who justifies the ungodly, his faith is reckoned as righteousness, just as David also speaks of the blessing upon man to whom GOD RECKONS RIGHTEOUS-NESS APART FROM WORKS.

Romans 4:1–6

. . . and hope does not disappoint, because the love of God has been poured out within our hearts through the Holy Spirit who was given to us.

Romans 5:5

And without becoming weak in faith he contemplated his own body, now as good as dead since he was about a hundred years old, and the deadness of Sarah's womb; yet WITH RESPECT TO THE PROMISE OF GOD, he did not waver in unbelief, but grew strong in faith, giving glory to God, and being fully assured that WHAT HE HAD PROMISED, HE WAS ABLE ALSO TO PERFORM.

Romans 4:19–21

What then is Apollos? And what is Paul? Servants through whom you believed, even as the Lord GAVE OPPORTUNITY TO EACH ONE. I planted, Apollos watered, but GOD WAS CAUSING THE GROWTH. So then neither the one who plants, nor the one who waters is anything, but GOD WHO CAUSES THE GROWTH.

1 Corinthians 3:5–7

Let no one keep defrauding you of your prize by delighting in self-abasement and the worship of the angels, taking his stand on visions he has seen, INFLATED WITHOUT CAUSE BY HIS FLESHLY MIND, and not holding fast to the head, from whom the entire body, being supplied and held together by the joints and ligaments, GROWS WITH A GROWTH WHICH IS FROM GOD.

Colossians 2:18,19

For by the grace you have been saved through faith; and that not of yourselves, IT IS THE GIFT OF GOD; not as a result of works, that no one should boast. For WE ARE HIS WORK- MANSHIP CREATED in Christ Jesus for good works, which God prepared beforehand, that we should walk in them.

Ephesians 2:8–10

Finally, be strong in the Lord, and IN THE STRENGTH OF HIS MIGHT.

Ephesians 6:10

And my God SHALL SUPPLY ALL YOUR NEEDS according to His riches in glory in Christ Jesus.

Philippians 4:19

And GOD IS ABLE to make all grace abound to you, that always having all sufficiency in everything, you may have an abundance for every good deed.

2 Corinthians 9:8

For indeed He was crucified because of weak- ness, yet He lives BECAUSE OF THE POWER

OF GOD. For we also are weak in Him, yet we shall live with Him BECAUSE OF THE POWER OF GOD DIRECTED TOWARD YOU.

2 Corinthians 13:4

He who did not spare His own Son, but delivered Him up for us all, how will He not also with Him FREELY GIVE US all things?

Romans 8:32

But when the fullness of the time came, GOD SENT forth His Son, born of a woman, born under the Law, in order that HE MIGHT REDEEM those who were under the Law, that WE MIGHT RECEIVE the adoption as sons.

Galatians 4:4,5

But Moses said to the people, "Do not fear! Stand by and see the salvation of the Lord WHICH HE WILL ACCOMPLISH FOR YOU today; for the Egyptians whom you have seen today, you will never see them again forever. The LORD WILL FIGHT FOR YOU while you keep silent."

Exodus 14:13,14

In the wilderness HE FED YOU manna which your fathers did not know, that He might humble you and that He might test you, to do good for you in the end. Otherwise, you may say in your heart, "My power and the

*strength of my hand made me this wealth."
But you shall remember the Lord your God,
FOR IT IS HE WHO IS GIVING YOU POWER
to make wealth, that He may confirm His cove-
nant which He swore to your fathers, as it is
this day.*

Deuteronomy 8:16–18

*GOD IS FAITHFUL, through whom you
were called into fellowship with His Son, Jesus
Christ our Lord.*

1 Corinthians 1:9

*FAITHFUL IS HE WHO CALLS YOU, and
HE ALSO WILL BRING IT TO PASS.*

1 Thessalonians 5:24

*For when God made the promise to Abra-
ham, since He could swear by no one greater,
He swore by Himself, saying, I WILL SURELY
BLESS YOU, AND I WILL SURELY MULTI-
PLY YOU.*

Hebrews 6:13,14

*No temptation has overtaken you but such
as it is common to man; AND GOD IS FAITH-
FUL, WHO WILL NOT ALLOW YOU to be
tempted beyond what you are able, but with
the temptation WILL PROVIDE THE WAY
OF ESCAPE ALSO, that you may be able to
endure it.*

1 Corinthians 10:13

Therefore, He had to be made like His breth-ren in all things, that He might become a merci-ful and faithful high priest in things pertain-ing to God, TO MAKE PROPITIATION FOR THE SINS OF THE PEOPLE.

Hebrews 2:17

NOT ONE OF THE GOOD PROMISES WHICH THE LORD HAD MADE TO THE HOUSE OF ISRAEL FAILED; ALL CAME TO PASS.

Joshua 21:45

For we shall surely die and are like water spilled on the ground which cannot be gathered up again. YET GOD DOES NOT TAKE AWAY LIFE, BUT PLANS WAYS SO THAT THE BANISHED ONE MAY NOT BE CAST OUT OF HIM.

2 Samuel 14:14

Do you not believe that I am in the Father, and the Father is in Me? The words that I say to you I do not speak on My own initiative, but the Father abiding in Me DOES HIS WORKS.

Believe Me that I am in the Father, and the Father in Me; otherwise BELIEVE ON AC-COUNT OF THE WORKS THEMSELVES.

Truly, truly, I say to you, he who believes in Me, THE WORKS THAT I DO SHALL HE DO ALSO; and GREATER WORKS than these shall he do; BECAUSE I GO to the Father.

And whatever you ask in my name, THAT WILL I DO, that the Father may be glorified in the Son.

If you ask Me anything in My name, I WILL DO IT.

John 14:10–14

Chapter 5

What Builds Personal Wonder?

The testimony of God working builds faith.

Ever so subtly we evade this truth. We say, "Just let our people see the need and they'll take action." Yet, when we probe into the matter, we often discover that not only did they see a need, they also saw God working in it.

"Go home to your people and report to them what great things the Lord has done for you, and how He had mercy on you" (Mark 5:19). Why? So a disciple could flaunt his faith; strut his stuff? Not at all. Rather, let there be a declaring that God is at work through His Son.

"And he went away and began to proclaim in Decapolis what great things Jesus had done for him; and everyone marveled." Do you know what would cure many church ailments? A good dose of marveling. We would come alive in our faith if we had some men in our pulpits who marvel at God. Bible classes are quick and sharp when lead to marvel.

Let's peek in on two, fundamentally, plain men of God: "Now as they observed the confidence of Peter and John, and understood that they were uneducated and untrained men, they were marveling, and began to recognize them as having been with Jesus" (Acts 4:13). Seeing and hearing about the activities of God motivates and constructs faith. "The righteousness of God is revealed from faith to faith; as it is written, 'But the righteous man shall live by faith'" (Rom. 1:17). The faith of one person is passed on to become the faith of another.

Peter and John found threats of crude punishment to be of little significance compared to what they had experienced at the feet of Jesus. "For we cannot stop speaking what we have seen and heard" (Acts 4:20). Neither what they had studied nor what they had memorized bore consequence. What they had witnessed aroused their faith. Their conviction would be declared. "And with great power the apostles were giving witness to the resurrection of the Lord Jesus, and abundant grace was upon them all" (Acts 4:33).

They were giving witness. Theories? Theology? Debate? Argumentation? None of these diseases. They were saying, "You can believe it because we are witnesses to the fact." The faith of some instilling faith in others.

One of the mightiest passages of God reveals the consistency of the concept. The telling of personal experience is intended to induce relationships with the Father, Son, and Holy Spirit. Listen to the common phraseology of the apostle in 1 John 1:1–4.

What was from the beginning, what we have heard, what we have seen with our eyes, what

*we behold and our hands handled, concerning
the Word of Life—and the life was manifested,
and we have seen and bear witness and proclaim to you the eternal life, which was with
the Father and was manifested to us.*

*What we have seen and heard we proclaim
to you also. That you also may have fellowship
with us; and indeed our fellowship is with
the Father, and with His Son Jesus Christ.
And these things we write, so that our joy may
be made complete.*

What we have studied and debated we tend to
keep. But what we see and hear of God's working
we feel compelled to tell. We feel. Nothing deep
and weird. We feel. We burn within, are urged.
We feel compelled, driven by insistent necessity
because the wick of our faith is lit.

Although several Scriptures have been used to
portray the nature of building faith, don't miss
the message of these very passages. They reveal
that common men stirred the invisible, supernatural nature of others by simply passing on what
they had seen and heard. It was extremely uncom-
plicated.

They told stories about Jesus the way our par-
ents and grandparents tell of events back in the
good old days. These men built faith by relating
to others the movement of God. This is the instruction and testimony of the Bible. The reason faith
is constructed at the hearing of the word is that
the word reveals God at work.

The disciples told their first-hand experiences.
We are to tell ours.

John's chapter concerning the woman at the well (John 4:2–42) ideally illustrates how faith is built via "telling what you've seen." Jesus and the woman exchanged small talk and then large talk. The lady was not trained in the area of "belief building." She was not planning to evangelize anyone. She was merely moved by what she had discovered.

And from that city many of the Samaritans believed in Him because of the word of the woman who testified, "He told me all of the things that I had done." So when the Samaritans came to Him, they were asking Him to stay with them; and He stayed there two days.

And many more believed because of His word; and they were saying to the woman, "It is no longer because of what you said that we believe, for we have heard for ourselves and know that this One is indeed the Savior of the World."

Of us He says, "But you are a chosen race, a royal priesthood, a holy nation, a people for God's own possession, that you may proclaim the excellence of Him who called you out of the darkness into His marvelous light" (1 Peter 2:9).

Proclaim His excellencies about His marvel. This inspires faith.

Abraham and Sarah were far too old to have a child. But Abraham knew that God could call into being that which doesn't exist . . . and God worked. This story is still told. And, it continues to build faith.

God parted the Red Sea so that His people, who had been forced into slavery, could become free. He pulled back the waters, dried the river bed of its mud and the nation crossed unharmed. This true story still builds faith.

Esther took a stand, hesitantly at first, and spoke up for the people of God. Her faith is one of the most inspiring stories of yesteryear. And though the scene took place centuries ago, it promotes faith within the human heart today.

Ezekiel had gone to preaching school looking forward to his first church. God took him out to the cemetery and said, "Here it is. Have at it." Such a sight. This is not what a student evangelist dreams about. But . . . because of the power of God and the simple faith of this ordinary man, the story breathes faith into men, women, and children—even now.

When we let God work and then tell how He did, faith is fashioned within the receivers of the good news.

Ray and Sandy Wallace wanted to enter a preacher-training school. They worked, re-worked, and re-reworked their budget, trying to make financial arrangements so they could attend. It never worked on paper. Late one night they made one final approach to the dilemma. Then they wadded up the papers with all their reasons for failure and frustration and declared, "We are going." God worked for them and they serve in a church in Colorado today. Knowing this builds our faith.

Two years ago our congregation contributed nearly $25,000 for missions. One year ago we prayed and fasted that God would respond. The contribution was over $46,000. This year we did the same thing; praying and fasting during the month of May. To our breath-taking surprise, the collection was nearly $100,000. Sharing this story builds faith . . . not in people . . . but in the working of God.

Bob Hare, a missionary behind the iron curtain for forty years, spoke to our assembly one cold, wintry February morning. As he tugged at our heartstrings with the warming news that we could buy Bibles for the Polish for $1 each, I was reminded that I had $131 in my billfold from a trip to Oregon the day before. I committed in my heart to give him $20 for twenty Bibles.

His message continued with wonders of God's hand. I doubled my ante.

Then an inner argument started in my conscience. "What's with the $40? What about the other 91?"

"Well, I need it. Forty is pretty good, you know. Ten percent would only be $13. So, 40 is good."

"But I could give the $131."

"But, I never have much to carry."

"Do you think God can't handle your needs?" Bob continued his sermon.

"Okay, I'll give the whole wad. I wonder if I should place it on the communion table and have others join in?"

"What if they don't and I'm left for a fool?"

"What, though, if they would? God give me a sign as to what to do."

"God . . . how will I know the sign?"

As we all stood for the invitation song, my Wendy was three rows from the front, sobbing and motioning for me to "come 'ere." She laid her head on my shoulder and broken-heartedly cried. "Daddy, I've got $60 at home. Would you make out a check for me and I'll pay you the $60 when we get home?" I said, "Watch what God is going to do."

I shared the past few moments of my inner wrestling, plus Wendy's response, with the congregation. I told that the check for $60 plus the $131 cash would be placed on the table. While we sang a song, if anyone wanted to join in, come down the aisles and let us build our altar for Poland on the communion table.

Immediately, hundreds filed by. The appearance was that of an ant farm. All was so orderly that it looked orchestrated . . . by God. When the singing ceased, we all stood in awe. A mountain of green bills and pastel checks were stacked so high that a few rolled off onto the floor.

God moved us to give over $4,000 that started out as $20 and a thought. This story builds faith because it reinforces one more time that He is able.

A church needed $3.5 million to purchase property and begin construction. They had $700,000 saved. To raise the $3.5 million they gave away the savings at $100,000 per month for seven months to their ministries, missions, and the poor. On the day of the big collection that church gathered $3,501,000.

In August of 1990 I sat in Cline Paden's office. As he took a phone call I listened to him explain the need to move toward Cuba, believing God would open the door soon. He expressed the belief that Castro would fall from Gorbachev's graces due to upheaval in Moscow. Four weeks later it was announced that Gorbachev had cut funds to Cuba.

Yes, we can dare to marvel, to wonder, to be in awe. We can reclaim that outrageous feeling that the newly established people of Acts 2 experienced.

My friend, Brennan, writes, "I asked for wonder, and he gave it to me. A Philistine will stand before a Claude Monet painting and pick his nose; a person filled with wonder will stand there fighting back the tears."

By and large, our world has lost its sense of wonder. We have grown up. We no longer catch our breath at the sight of a rainbow or the scent of a rose, as we once did. We have grown bigger and everything else smaller, less impressive. We get blasé and worldly wise and sophisticated. We no longer run our fingers through water, no longer shout at the stars or make faces at the moon. Water is H_2O, the stars have been classified, and the moon is not made of green cheese. Thanks to satellite TV and jet planes, we can visit places available in the past only to, a Columbus, a Balboa, and other daring explorers.[9]

We must be possessed by His wonder. Restore this and we will relinquish our self-preserving defenses that hold off the loving works of God.

The worn phrase is still a good one, "Let go and let God." Fear plays havoc with our faith the way Paul did with the early church. Hearts want to believe that God is active . . . but.

God is so extremely willing. As Steve and Annie Chapman sing, "God still moves." God is awesome. So be awed!

Believe He labors; expect Him to . . . trust Him to be there.

Twice a year I play baseball in a special camp. Businessmen get to spend a little time in their field of dreams. Former Saint Louis Cardinal stars conduct the workouts as our coaches and then we play against them on the final day of camp. I became involved in this as a ministry. God has worked.

One summer weekend we were to work out in Busch Stadium on Friday and Saturday. Sunday was to be the big game against Al Hrabosky, Curt Flood, Bob Gibson, Joe Cunningham, Randy Hundley, Mike Tyson, Ted Savage, Gene Oliver, and other stars.

The Friday practice was great. But no opportunity to do kingdom work was apparent. I love the game. I love these men more. I look for any chance to convey encouragement to the stars and the rookies.

Because nothing special happened during practice, I felt a little empty and a little wasteful. In my hotel room, later, I prayed that God would open doors because I couldn't. Soon afterward I was headed over to Joe Cunningham's office. It occurred to me that I might possibly take my sons,

Dusty and Tim, down on the field before the game.

When I inquired, Joe gave me a special pass. I was to bring the boys to his office at 5:10 P.M. where we would meet a photographer who would accompany us.

I was thrilled!

Not because of the fun. Not just because our friend, Joe, had once again befriended us. It was certain . . . God was going to open a door for our ministry. By faith it was a fact. I raced to my room to tell Mary and the kids what had happened—from the unproductive practice, to the prayer, to the pass. I waved the pass in the air and said, "I don't know what this means. I know for sure it is an open door."

5:10 P.M. was good to us. We were escorted to the field. The Cardinals were all at the batting cage. Therefore, the dugout was empty. We were told that we'd spend about fifteen minutes in the dugout and then leave. If a player happened by, the boys might get an autograph and/or their picture taken. (The boys did meet Tom Nieto and Ozzie Smith.)

Time passed. Nothing I had assumed happened. Nothing. And then . . .

As we were leaving, one of the players leaned his bat against the cage and headed for the clubhouse. Our paths were perfectly timed to intersect. Of twenty-four active players on the roster, I had written one of them for two years, sowing the seed by faith in case I ever met him. This was the man. I knew this was it.

I said, "Oh, Darrell Porter, I have got to meet

you. I'm Terry Rush from Tulsa." His first words
were, "You write the most encouraging letters I've
ever received and I really mean that. I hope you
haven't written me lately as I haven't had time
to answer my mail."

When Darrell learned that I had written asking
if I could go to chapel with him and the team, he
invited me to go with him Sunday morning. That
was the door the Spirit of God afforded. We went
to chapel. I sat between John Tudor and Todd
Worrell. Afterwards, Darrell introduced me to
their chaplain, Walt Enoch.

As a result of that Friday's prayer and the be-
hind-the-scenes work of the Spirit of Christ, Mr.
Enoch allowed me to speak in chapel to the Cardinals, the Reds, and the Cubs.

We will see the goodness and the graciousness
of God if we will but come out from those dark
caves of fear. It is the Spirit who handles. It is
He alone that arranges. No wonder many have
an anemic prayer-life. We fear that God works,
and simultaneously we fear that He doesn't. Faith
knows, beyond the ability to know (Eph. 3:19),
that He does.

"I would have despaired unless I had believed
that I would see the goodness of the Lord in the
land of the living. Wait for the Lord; be strong;
and let your heart take courage; yes, wait for the
Lord" (Psalms 27:13,14).

There are inexhaustible treasures of resources
and supplies . . . invisibly true . . . for our faith
walk. Such is verifiable, not by logic, but by faith.

"For whatever is born of God overcomes the world; and this is the victory that has overcome the world—our faith. And who is the one who overcomes the world, but he who believes that Jesus is the Son of God" (1 John 5:4,5).

Chapter 6

Testimonies of God Working

In this chapter you will read true-life stories that demonstrate how God works through the faith of believers. These are just a few of the testimonies that have been shared with me over the years.

About a month ago I was watching a "Special" on television about the hostages in Lebanon. I hate to admit this, but I've never thought too much about the situation. I've seen headlines in the newspaper and heard bits and pieces on the news, but this special program had quite an impact on me.

A few of us are meeting on Saturday mornings to pray for any and all things. I *had* to pray for these hostages. In the days to come the girls in the prayer group also prayed. It wasn't any time at all before the first hostage was released . . . then the second. We're now looking for the next release(s) as God works it out. I don't know how He did it, I just know He did it and that He's

going to take care of it. And, of course, we know
hundreds of other people have been praying for
these releases to occur. It is so wonderful to be a
part of answered prayer. It is so exciting, and what
motivation to continue in prayerful fellowship with
Him! What is He going to do next? I don't want
to miss out on seeing Him work his wonders.

Jan Shackleford
Tulsa, Oklahoma

One of the fundamental principles that has
guided the work of the World Bible Translation
Center in Fort Worth over the years is the belief
that a person does not have the Scriptures until
he has them in a form he can understand and a
style that dynamically conveys the original message.

In 1981, after prayerful consideration of Russian
as a new target language, translation was begun
on what would become the New Century Russian
Version (NCRV) in modern Russian. Almost immediately two questions were raised: "Why translate
into Russian?" and, "What will you be able to do
with it when it is finished?"

The first question was not difficult to answer.
The most recent translation or revision of the Au-
thorized Russian Text, The Holy Synod Version,
was completed in 1864. There have been many
changes in the Russian language since then that
make it difficult to be understood by the common
man in Russia today. Howard Clark Kee of Boston
University is quoted as saying, "(Russian) church
authorities told us there's an enormous pressure

at all levels for a Bible that's not just a sacred object, but something to be read." The second question was a bit more difficult. The response was simply, "We don't know."

A well qualified Russian national, married to an American merchant seaman, was located living near the center. Translation work was begun and moving along nicely when, without prior notice one Friday, the lady announced that her husband had been transferred to Washington state and she was moving to be with him the following week. When queried about why she had not given prior notice, she explained that she just could not bear to think of the problem her moving would cause since she was unable to recommend anyone to take her place. She was asked to do all she could to try to locate someone suitable. The Translation Center staff united in prayer for God's guidance in selecting a replacement so that the work could be continued.

A few days later the phone rang and a lady enquired about the possibility of there being an opening for a Russian translator. It was surmised that this was a referral from the first translator and she was invited to come in for an interview. She turned out to be better qualified than the first lady. Amazingly, she had noted the center listing while thumbing through the Yellow Pages of the Phone Book. Coincidence?

Years passed and the tedious job of translating the Gospels, the Epistles and the remainder of the New Testament from the original Greek neared

completion. It was finished during the Spring of
1988, the year of the millennial celebration of the
Russian Orthodox Church when President Gorbachev opened the way for free importation of the
Scriptures into the Soviet Union for the first time
in decades. What was begun in 1981 was completed
the year the doors were opened. What Divine timing!

In August 1989 under the title GOOD NEWS
FROM GOD, the first copies of the NCRV New
Testament rolled off the press. Ten thousand copies were immediately sent to Russia with the
prayer that they would clear customs and that it
would be possible to distribute them to those
attending the Moscow International Book Fair.
They did clear customs and thousands stood in
line to receive their copy of God's Word. The
10,000 copies were soon exhausted. More than
17,000 people left their names and addresses on
pieces of paper. Their Testaments were sent by
registered mail from Moscow. Hundreds of letters have been received, many expressing appreciation for their New Testaments and thousands enquiring about where and how copies can
be obtained.

Translation of the Old Testament was begun
in 1988. It is scheduled for completion in 1991.
It is estimated that each copy will be read and
cherished by ten Soviet citizens.

What an unparalleled opportunity God is providing with His promise, recorded by the Prophet
Isaiah, "My word will not return to me void" or,

as translated in the New Century Easy to Read Version in modern English: "My words make things happen that I want to happen. My words succeed in doing the things I send them to do. My words will go out with happiness, and they will bring peace" (55:11,12). God's timing is perfect, His goodness is beyond measure and His provision unlimited!

>Marvin R. Steffins
>Special Assistant to the President
>World Bible Translation Center
>Fort Worth, Texas

Some time ago, I returned to a community where I had previously preached. When I checked into my motel room, on the dresser was a beautiful arrangement of flowers and on the table an enormous basket of fruit. I read the enclosed note attached to the flowers and it said, "Because of what you've meant to us."

I immediately looked up the number of the couple who had signed the note and expressed my appreciation but was unsure what I had done. I asked, "What in the world have I done for you?"

"Oh," the man replied, "You and a doctor saved my life."

Well, this was very interesting and humbling and I pressed him to tell me the story. He explained, "Some years ago I had a stroke which was a great blow to me. It rendered my left side paralyzed and interfered with the left side of my mouth and disturbed my speech. I lay in bed and thought, 'I am just a remnant of a man. I don't amount to anything anymore. I have had it. I am all through.' "

"But the doctor insisted I go through physical therapy. I slowly recovered though my heart wasn't in it. One day he came to see me and said, 'You are much better. Your reactions are improved. If you would improve your attitude and believe you can get well, you would completely recover.' "

A wise doctor, for equally important as medicine is your will to get well. That doctor knew that this man would need a mighty will and dose of faith because he had a mighty mountain in front of him. So he told him, "If you make up your mind and believe in your heart that you can, you can get out of bed, complete therapy, and return to work."

His wife had recently secured a copy of my new book, *Dynamic Living for Difficult Days*. She gave it to him to read. He read a chapter in it that talks of "having faith as a grain of mustard seed . . . nothing will be impossible for you" (Matthew 17:20). He thought, "I believe that." But didn't really; he only thought he did; he didn't really believe it would work in his case.

But a few days later, his wife came and pulled back the bed covers and said, "Get out of bed. Are you a man or a worm? Put your hand in mine and think of what the Lord Jesus Christ said and get out of that bed."

She knew what she was doing. He put his foot down gingerly. "I followed her," he told me, "in a staggering fashion to the door of my room. There she let go of my hand and she said, 'Now go on your own. But remember, Jesus Christ will hold you up.' I looked at her and I knew she believed it and suddenly I did too."

The next day that man came up to me at the church building and hugged me. He thanked me again for prompting him to believe in something greater than himself. When he walked away, all I could see of anything special was a slight limp of the left leg. His words rang in my ears, "I got my life back and have some wonderful opportunities because I learned to believe."

Faith can indeed lift you up—and hold you up.

Douglas F. Parsons
Midland, Texas

My sons' Senior year of High School was a trying time in itself. Being a single parent, struggling with Senior expenses, which football scholarships should he choose and how were we going to make it to the middle, let alone make the ends meet. But through the Faith of our Lord, my family knew it would happen. We were broke. And in addition to this . . .

Pure Panic. I just sat down and cried and began to pray that Brian was ok. Soon I felt this hand on my shoulder. "Mom" came this voice, "I am sorry I wrecked the car."

Like all good mothers, after you see your young out of danger—well you want to put them back in danger with that "Mother Look." I was on the verge of hostility. And this 6' 6" kid says, "Mom, God will take care of it all for us." At that moment

I really didn't see God taking care of anything except lying to me that "If you follow me, I will give you rest." Nightmares are not rest in my book! Sunday, Rachel and Brian got ready for church. I didn't, I wouldn't go to church or have anything to do with it. My anger was still raging inside me. I sat in the living room alone, crying, literally screaming at God. "I promised you I would try to be a good Christian and raise the children to love you. Why have you let me down?" I felt like Christ on the cross. "My God, My God why have you forsaken me."

Being the person I am, I just screamed at God "If you want me back in the church Big Boy, you give me a sign that I am yours and you really do love us."

The phone rings. Our youth minister, Tracy Ellis, says "Mom Deckman, Teressa and I will come and get you for church." I told him "No way! I am not going. I am not going to have people say 'How are you?' When they don't even care or mean it. I am not going to say I am fine. I am not fine, I am ill! I won't be back to church!" Tracy, as loving as he is, says "Mom Deckman, we love you and Teressa has some stew for you and we want to bring it by after church." So I agreed.

7:15 P.M. the knock on the door. I told Rachel to let Tracy in. But no Tracy, our teens from church began filing in and telling me "Mom we love you and everything will be all right." Finally, I hear Tracy's voice, "Hey Mom Deckman." "We all can't fit in your apartment." "Why don't you come out here?"

I walked out with teens still hugging and stuffing money in the pockets of my jeans. As I walked out 80 Angels are singing "We Love You with the Love of The Lord." My heart felt so warm, I can't tell you the joy it was that the Church came to me. I told God to send me a sign, and He sent showers of blessings. How awesome can my God be to forgive me and send his 80 angels to restore my faith.

One young man, Bobby Lott, came over and said he wanted to speak with me alone. So, off we go over by his car. Bobby hands me the keys to his car and says the car is mine. Now we are talking a 17 year old giving up his wheels. The rest of the teens, and adults gave up allowances, lunch money, tax refunds, money for a new suit and much more than that, they gave my family their love of God and restored my faith. GOD WILL TAKE CARE OF YOU!

Linda Deckman
Tulsa, Oklahoma

I joined International Expeditions in the Summer of 1979 at a time when world-wide interest in the search for the Ark of Noah was increasing and the prospects of producing a feature documentary film seemed to be a viable investment opportunity. However, political unrest in Turkey together with the hostage crisis in neighboring Iran made it impossible to proceed with the search until 1982.

Earlier, in the Summer of 1978, Apollo Astronaut Colonel Jim Irwin had accompanied an International Expeditions team to Turkey to search for the Ark. Much time was consumed in the bureaucratic process to obtain permits and the expedition was eventually canceled. However, before returning to the States Colonel Irwin accepted an invitation to share his experience on the moon with Turkish General Kenan Evren and his officers. He presented the General with a special gift, a Turkish flag that he had taken to the moon.

In 1982, General Evren, now President of Turkey, offered the use of military aircraft for the search. I accompanied Jim and a team to Turkey. Plans to use the plane were frustrated, however, when it was learned that President Evren had gone to Yugoslavia for holiday and no one on the General Staff was prepared to accept responsibility for authorizing the use of the aircraft that the president had promised. Because of impending bad weather, the decision was made to attempt a climb to check out a report of a sighting that had been made earlier in the Summer. It proved to be more difficult than anticipated with the equipment available so we returned to the States hoping to return immediately with the necessary equipment and personnel.

The prospect of searching for the Ark, God's way of salvation for Noah and his family at the time of the great flood, carried with it the possibility of sharing Good News about Christ as revealed in the New Testament, the way of salvation for all mankind today.

It was with this mission in mind that, late in the Summer of 1982, we witnessed the first of three exceptional answers to prayer for provision of funds and direction to continue our search in Turkey.

The Sunday following our return from Turkey, at a Missions Conference in Sugarland, Texas, I shared my enthusiasm about confirming discovery of the Ark of Noah and asked those present to join me in prayer for direction and provision. Facing the possibility of inclement fall weather closing in, it was important if, in fact, we were going to return, that we leave immediately, the following week. $15,000 was needed to do this.

Monday morning I phoned Bill, a long time friend in Houston, and asked him to join us in prayer for the necessary funding. He did and stunned us before the end of the day by arranging to provide the $15,000! Bill joined us as we left for Turkey the next day with the necessary equipment, a team of experienced climbers and a lot of enthusiasm. However, there were unexpected delays so that when we got on the mountain, before we reached the site, bad weather set in and the expedition had to be postponed again.

We made plans to begin earlier the following Summer with a team that would eventually number more than thirty on the mountain. We were scheduled to leave on a Tuesday in July. The preceding Friday we still lacked $15,000.

I sat at my desk praying and preparing to phone team members to cancel the expedition. The phone rang. It was Kenneth, a godly friend calling from Purley, England to enquire about how our plans were progressing. He offered to wire transfer the needed $15,000. However, he was six hours ahead of us in England, and the banks were about to close. Funds just could not be transferred in time to make the departure deadline the following Tuesday. I thanked him, hung up somewhat confused, praying for God's guidance. The phone rang again. This time it was Don, a friend in the insurance business calling from Memphis to tell me that he had just won a sales contest, a weekend in London. He was leaving that afternoon with his daughter Paige. They would return on Monday. It took only a matter of minutes, with a return call to Ken in England, to arrange for Don to pick up the funds and return with them in time for our scheduled departure for Eastern Turkey.

We proceeded to Turkey. We arranged for the use of a fixed wing military aircraft and flew over the area several times where the object was supposed to have been sighted. We saw nothing that resembled the remains of the Ark of Noah. We checked several other areas. Subsequent climbs to view these locations were unproductive. Once again our time ran out and inclement weather made it impossible to complete the search. We knew where the Ark was not! We left Turkey with the prospect of using a helicopter in 1984 to complete the search.

Early in the Spring of 1984 we applied for permit to use a helicopter. No government response. We enquired further. No answer. Finally, just a few days before scheduled departure, we received the go-ahead. When cost of the copter was added to the amount we had budgeted, there was a $15,000 shortfall.

It was at this point that Clyde, a long-time friend and President of an electronics firm in Indiana, phoned to enquire about how our plans were progressing. He indicated that their Board had just met and voted to make a contribution of $4,000 with the offer of a non-interest bearing loan for $10,000 for three years. I expressed my deep appreciation to him but advised that I was forbidden to borrow money to finance the expedition. He said he would go back to the board. A few minutes later the phone rang again. It was Dr. John, a member of our 1984 Expedition team calling from California. He said that he had just received a commitment of $10,000 earmarked for the helicopter! A few minutes later the phone rang and it was Clyde again. He said his board had voted to increase their contribution to five thousand dollars. For the third consecutive year, our need of $15,000 had been met just hours before time of departure.

Results and reports of the 1984 expedition to the site of "boat" in the Mountains of Ararat have been broadcast, televised and printed by news media around the world. World attention has been focused, again and again, on the Genesis record of the flood, on Noah, the preacher of righteousness, on God's provision and His timing—never mere coincidence.

"Depend on the Lord. Trust Him, He will do what must be done" (Psalm 37:5). His promise is sure and as wise King Solomon wrote: "Always turn to the Lord for help in everything you do,

and you will be successful" (Proverbs 16:3; Easy-
to-Read Translation).

> Marvin R. Steffins
> President
> International Expeditions, Inc.

Chapter 7

Where Will Faith Lead?

As surely as the word of God proclaims good news, warnings are also a part of its precious cargo. The Way is so vital that counterproductive ways are continually introduced by the slight of the devil's hand. "For such men are false apostles; deceitful workers, disguising themselves as apostles of Christ. And no wonder, for even Satan disguises himself as an angel of light" (2 Cor. 11:13,14).

Satan opposes God. The visible contrasts the unseen. Death confronts life. Sin resists righteousness. Lies counter truth. And, fear mocks faith. Not only must we explore routes to build believing hearts; we must alert seekers to potential conflicting channels designed to destroy. Usually these adversaries look and/or sound right.

Charles Swindoll describes these angels of light as clean-living, nice-looking, law-abiding citizens, so highly respected that we would never guess we are living next door to killers.

They kill freedom, spontaneity, and creativity; they kill joy as well as productivity. They kill with their words and their pens and their looks. They kill with their attitudes far more often than with their behavior. There is hardly a church or Christian organization or Christian school or missionary group or media ministry where such danger does not lurk. The amazing thing is that they get away with it, day in and day out, without being confronted or exposed. Strangely, the same ministries that would not tolerate heresy for ten minutes will step aside and allow these killers all the space they need to maneuver and manipulate others in the most insidious manner imaginable. Their intolerance is tolerated. Their judgmental spirits remain unjudged. Their bullying tactics continue unchecked. And their narrow-mindedness is either explained away or quickly defended. The bondage that results would be criminal were it not so subtle and wrapped in such spiritual-sounding garb.[10]

Their household slogans have ravaged and raped hearts of faith, leaving believers wounded beyond repair. Disciples' desires to launch into the deep have been torpedoed by well-chosen phrases that eventually bring one's hope to wearied ruin. Beware of the dogs that howl until we no longer assemble to unite our faith, but, rather, assemble to unite our fears.

Dallas Willard accurately states:

In other words, Paul and his Lord were people of immense power, who saw clearly the way-

ward ways of the world considered natural.
With calm premeditation and clear vision of
a deeper order, they took their stand always
among those "last who shall be first" men-
tioned repeatedly in the Gospels. With their
feet slanted in the deeper order of God, they
lived lives of utter self-sacrifice and abandon-
ment, seeing in such a life the highest possible
personal attainment.

And through that way of living God gave
them "the power of an indestructible life" (Hebrews 7:16) to accomplish the work of their
appointed ministry and to raise them above
the power of death. During their lives, they
both were men of lowly and plain origin and
manner, when compared with the glittering
and glamorous ones who dominated the
world's attention. So most of their powerful
contemporaries could not possibly have seen
either of them for who they were. Nor can
we, until we have begun in faith actually to
live as they lived.[11]

Faith Needs to Go Beyond . . .

Five Steps to the Plan of Salvation

Out of the Restoration Movement came the five
steps of salvation, which coincide with the fingers
on one's hand. Hear, believe, repent, confess, and
be baptized remain the basic approach. Although,
this approach is true, it is not all of truth.

A blinding hindrance has developed from this

rote approach. First, baptism has evolved into a goal much like a sales figure targeted by a group for the end of the month: be baptized and the plan has been fulfilled. But baptism is not the end. It is not the accumulation of the other four steps, with this final step bringing response to completion.

Bible baptism is the beginning of life—not the end. We are to be born again. We are recreated by the Holy Spirit at baptism. Although, many would agree, their practice and their speech betray them. Baptism becomes the pursuit, rather than fellowship with God.

Ask many, who have completed the final five, what is next in the line of responsibility for a Christian. There is a consistent uncertainty coupled, sadly, with disinterest. This notion of baptism being the high rung in the salvation ladder leaves a person wet and with nowhere to go . . . except to church . . . with little depth or meaning.

Second, this five-step system confines faith to the second interval. Belief has been restricted to stage #2. Remember that baptism has been our goal. The word calls for baptized believers. We are seeing immersed ones who do not believe God can work, direct, nor handle life.

It is not uncommon to counsel a Christian who was buried in baptism yet fears he is lost. Such is baptism without faith. Faith was, not in God, but in the meaning and method of baptism. Thus, assurance of salvation is tragically surrendered. Many don't feel this way. Be warned and beware of those who do.

Faith Needs to Go Beyond . . .

"God Gave Us a Brain for Common Sense"

God gives us the freedom to choose between the seen and unseen, between temporary and permanent truths. Common sense won't fly. Its bark is big, but its wisdom comes from below. Abraham went out not knowing where he was going (Heb. 11:8). That's not good logic. But it was amazing faith and it was pleasing to God.

Jesus shared a secret with Peter. The Son was headed for Jerusalem to be killed by the mob. In the name of logic, Peter rebuked Him. In the name of God, Jesus pointed out a major flaw in such thinking—it was based on the use of the brain God gave him. Peter had chosen to set it on man's interests, not Jehovah's.

> *Now when Jesus was in Bethany at the home of Simon the leper, a woman came to Him with an alabaster vial of very costly perfume, and she poured it upon His head as He reclined at the table. But the disciples were indignant when they saw this, and said, "Why this waste? For this perfume might have been sold for a high price and the money given to the poor"* (Matt. 26:6–9).

In the name of reason why didn't she use her head? In the name of religion why didn't she realize her stewardship responsibilities?

In the name of love she lost her head and gave her heart.

Faith Needs to go Beyond . . .

"Where Will All of This Lead?"

When someone asks "Where will all this lead?" the battle between faith and fear is imminent. The issue is not obedience to Scripture. The issue is control. Yielding and surrendering are flannelgraph words for Bible class. Control is the name of the game. When we don't know where a move will lead, when we can't control where a move will lead, fear quenches faith. Fear is lethal.

Spontaneity scares faithless people. If it would have been up to us we would have had only three baptized on the day of Pentecost, rather than three thousand, so the people could have opportunity to get used to the idea. We fear God can't handle His own creation . . . or His own growth patterns. Do we not work at our pace instead of His?

We must surrender so that God can move. "The wind blows where it wishes and you hear the sound of it, but do not know where it comes from and where it is going; so is everyone who is born of the Spirit" (John 3:8). So is the Holy Spirit? No. So is everyone born of the Spirit.

James and John felt the need to take control when the Samaritans refused hospitality to Jesus. "And when His disciples James and John saw this, they said, 'Lord, do you want us to command fire to come down from heaven and consume them?' But He turned and rebuked them, and said, 'You do not know what kind of spirit you are of; for the Son of Man did not come to destroy men's lives, but to save them'" (Luke 9:54–56).

Beware anytime an answer can be given to the question, "Where will all of this lead?" If there is an answer, the issue may only be of sight. To walk by faith and not by sight emphatically implies that the trail cannot be seen. That's the point. God's leadership will take us so far out of sight that success fades into His glory (Eph. 3:20,21).

The very question implies, "Show me and I'll consider going." Yet, we are called to go, not seeing, but believing. That's Abraham's example in Romans 4:16–21 and again in Hebrews 11:8.

Faith Needs to Go Beyond . . .

"We Better Play It Safe."

Playing it safe is what Moses deeply desired to do when God called him to lead the captives out of Egypt. "Just to be safe, God, you better pick somebody else."

Playing it safe was the philosophy of ten of the twelve spies. God didn't want safety, He wanted faith. God didn't ask that an opinion poll be taken. He made a promise, but they weren't too sure about the security system.

The third slave who hid his one talent did so in the name of playing it safe. The master called him wicked and lazy. Those are the characteristics of playing it safe. It's wicked because it restricts the grace of God. And, too, it is evil because it enormously hinders faith that others want to express. It's lazy because it just doesn't want to bother with risk and uncertainty.

"Anyone who goes too far and does not abide in the teaching of Christ, does not have God; the one who abides in the teaching, he has both the Father and the Son" (2 John 9). Faith's call is to abide by the instructions and the promises. We aren't called to run a credit check on His call. Rather, we are expected to take Him at His word with full trust.

We don't play it safe . . . we are safe. "What then shall we say to these things? If God is for us, who is against us? He who did not spare His own Son, but delivered Him up for us all, how will He not also with Him freely give us all things" (Rom. 8:31,32).

Faith Needs to Go Beyond . . .

"This Move Will Stir up Trouble."

Faith makes a sudden move to cut up through the gap only to be tackled viciously from behind. How many attempts at letting God roam through our streets with love and grace are stifled by the fear that such a tactic might cause trouble in the church. We need to admit one thing: Jesus spells trouble. Jesus is the "C" word . . . controversial.

Elder, if you don't want battle, persecution, and even bloodshed, don't hang around this man. Preacher, if you aren't prepared for assault, slander, stress, and challenge, you aren't prepared to preach. The reputation of Jesus . . . and His followers . . . is fiercely consistent: it is trouble.

If leadership wants to know one reason why

we get a "C" or maybe a "C+" for church growth
it is because of our hesitancy to confront those
who insist we walk by their sight. We should not
look for a fight. Jesus didn't. But his commitment
to an invisible God forced it. Faith will conflict
with fear—especially when fear runs the church.
Let it be clear; Jesus rocked the religious boat.

*Blessed are those who have been persecuted
for the sake of righteousness, for theirs is the
kingdom of heaven. Blessed are you when men
cast insults at you, and persecute you, and
say all kinds of evil against you falsely, on
account of Me. Rejoice, and be glad, for so
they persecuted the prophets who were before
you* (Matt. 5:10–12).

*Do not think I came to bring peace on the
earth; I did not come to bring peace but a
sword. For I came to set a man against his
Father, and a daughter against her Mother,
and a daughter-in-law against her mother-in-
law; and a man's enemies will be members
of his household* (Matt. 10:34–36).

*You men who are stiff-necked and uncircum-
cised in heart and ears are always resisting
the Holy Spirit; you are doing just as your
fathers did. Which one of the prophets did your
fathers not persecute?* (Acts 7:51,52).

Our unity is to be based on the Spirit, not on
whatever keeps the herd from being restless. Faith

is betrayed when we spend more effort pacifying unbelieving critics than we do pleasing God. How many times has faith been dimmed because some good soul was worried over what the brotherhood would think?

Are we to love the brotherhood? Of course. Are we to be interested in it? Yes. However, we are neither called to obey it nor to worship it. We are not our own god. We are neither our own ruler nor our own leader. He alone is the One.

"For to you it has been granted for Christ's sake, not only to believe in Him, but also to suffer for His sake, experiencing the same conflict which you saw in me, and now hear to be in me" (Phil. 1:29,30).

Faith will breathe deeper if we will be honest in our devotion to God, rather than persistently craving to keep men happy. God warns us about pleasing men.

Faith Needs to Go Beyond . . .

The Look

Have you ever been firmly convicted about the unseen, only to have hope drained out of you by . . . the look? This may sound elementary, and even silly, to you, but this segment is warranted. Too, it is revealed in Scripture.

"You foolish Galatians, who has bewitched you, before whose eyes Jesus Christ was publicly portrayed as crucified? This is the only thing I want to find out from you: did you receive the Spirit by the works of the Law, or by hearing with faith? Are you so foolish? Having begun by the Spirit, are you now being perfected by the flesh?" (Gal. 3:1–3).

Bewitched: to give one the evil eye. Remember, as a child, when you told company at the dinner table what your mother specifically told you not to mention? And do you remember how she was so calm on the outside and had that guilt/embarrassed smile, but on the inside she was pinching your neck off? She bewitched you!

That woman sent you a loaded message. It was loud. Nobody got the word but you. You were the only one being bewitched. Without a word those squinted eyes said, "I promise you that when these people go home I'll get you. Sure these relatives are saving you now. But, believe me I won't forget. Never. You'll be sorry. You just wait. I'm not going to tell you what's going to happen to you now, but believe me when I tell you, you are going to get it. Do you hear me?"

And she said all that without even taking a breath. It was a silent message. Her eyes did the talking.

It has happened at the table. It happened to the Galatians. And, it still happens in the church. The knees of faith have been buckled by the glare of the brother and the stare of the sister that said, "How dare you preach on that topic," or "You better not teach against my traditions in this class," or "You're in big trouble, Buster."

Faith is the element within the Christian that

satisfies God. Be certain it is targeted for delay and destruction. Be kind, humble, gentle, and sensitive to people . . . always. At the same time, do not yield to another what is rightfully God's . . . your faith.

Gynnath Ford wrote the following:

"I want to change, but people might criticize me." Good. Let them criticize!

Coretta King, widow of the late Martin Luther King, answered the critics who believed blacks were inferior. "I knew I was not inferior, because nobody ever goes to such lengths to oppress or to retard a basically inferior person."

My friend Neil Gallagher says, "Attacks do not come to garbage dumps, but to jewelry stores." You are not garbage. You are a diamond!

A politician did the best job he could. He made mistakes and was criticized severely. The objections contained grave errors. He visited a friend in the country and asked his advice. The farmer could scarcely hear the story because his hound dog was barking at the full moon. The farmer told the dog to stop, but he kept on howling.

The farmer answered the politician. "You want to know how to answer the critics. Listen to that dog. Look at the moon. Remember, people will keep howling at you. They will snap at you and criticize you. But here's the answer: The dogs keep howling, but the moon keeps shining."

Jesus, the best man who ever lived, was criticized. You will be too.

"Power to Become"

Faith needs to go beyond the moments of hesitation. Slogans and reasons and excuses bombard the business meetings unanimously designed to leave faith in a mess. We have sold the farm. The belief system has been taken captive by scare tactics . . . and these tactics have worked.

We are political. We are dishonest. We love the applause of men. Faith released will thrust us into the hottest of all kitchens. I'm saying we will endure!

Chapter 8

Aim for Bigger Faith

Assistance with the sticky wickets of life is available if we simply trust the work of God. God does make a difference. Faith is a stabilizing factor. As spiritual awareness progresses, the personality that was characterized by calamity evolves to one characterized by calmness. Disposition improves.

Beware of dead-end alleys. Book learning isn't the answer. Potential often misfires. Countries are full of miserable and wrecked people, who were once heralded as having great potential. Interference abruptly curtails intended plans, and ideas are often aborted. Faith can (note this) see us through. It changes not only our outlook, but our look. "Therefore if any man is in Christ, he is a new creature; the old things passed away; behold, new things have come" (2 Corin. 5:17).

Faith Offers Peace

"Therefore having been justified by faith, we have peace with God through our Lord Jesus Christ" (Rom. 5:1).

79

How does one cultivate tranquility when we still
have to pay car insurance, go to wedding showers,
visit the dentist and keep the chain letters going
with the IRS? Can it be done? Heaven help us!
And that's the point. Heaven helps.

Begin by believing that attaining peace is God's
will for us. Jesus calls common folk to relax. "Come
to Me, all who are weary and heavy-laden, and I
will give you rest" (Matt. 11:28). The Holy Spirit
indwells the truster while bearing the fruit of peace
(Gal. 5:22). Phobia that would ordinarily drive one
to destruction can be dissolved. Higher concentration on the Highest Reality brings about answers
and solutions.

Worry infects our aim and focus. Fear often insists that we not trust anyone but ourselves to
get a job done. Such thinking drives us insane
because it spreads us too thinly. We wonder what
good it does to believe in the ability of God.

"So then it does not depend on the man who
wills or the man who runs, but on God who has
mercy" (Rom. 9:16). God can handle through others
what we prefer to keep for ourselves, but are too
tired to do.

Faith ushers in dependence on God. God desires
dependence. As a matter of fact, He insists on it.
Relinquish selfish control. Accept the efforts of others. Thank God. And rest.

Buttons and bumper stickers make the bold comment: *Lead, Follow or Get out of the Way.* That's
somewhat smug. Such an admonition could have
been expressed by the reckless apostle Peter when
he crudely elbowed his way into the empty tomb

of Jesus. The insinuation is that if you'll get out of the way, along with all the rest of the ignorant and lazy people, someone will get on with the project at hand.

The way to peace is to get ourselves out of the way. Believe that God works and then get out of the way so He can. You will receive peace.

Faith Calls for Courage

Taking risks is a huge component of faith. To go where we cannot see is a great venture. Faith takes risks; sight plays it safe.

Chance. Venture. Hazard. Gambling. Jeopardy. Danger. Peril. Uncertainty. Insecurity. Exposure. Vulnerability. Apprehension. Trap. Pitfall. Ambush.

Dangerous course. Leap in the dark. Road to ruin. Cause for alarm. Source of danger. Brewing storm. Odds against you. Gathering clouds.

Run a risk. Be open to criticism. Set yourself up for trouble. Run for it. Hang by a thread. Live in a glass house. Play with fire. Skate on thin ice.

These words and phrases describe the winds that blew into the face of Jesus. They storm upon us, too. Jesus was and is a risk. Followers must have courage. Religion will accommodate pretenders. Christianity, though, sorts the sheep from the goats. Disciples dare while philosophers talk and doubters gossip.

Jesus walked an unsafe path. He was called on the carpet. Jesus talked a life that was misunderstood. He was sent to jail and railroaded as guilty. Jesus was mislabeled. He died.

"Be strong and courageous! Do not tremble or be dismayed, for the Lord your God is with you wherever you go" (Josh. 1:9).

"Finally, be strong in the Lord, and in the strength of his might. Put on the full armor of God, that you may be able to stand firm against the schemes of the devil" (Eph. 6:10,11).

Faith Is Fearless

Fear is spiritual polio. It may not kill our faith, but it will certainly keep us out of the gym and out of the race. It removes us from all competition. Fear's paralysis reduces us from participants to spectators.

"You believe that God is one. You do well; the demons also believe, and shudder" (James 2:19). Believing and shuddering. Stay away from this strange combination. More than just being possible, it is quite common to have just enough faith in God to be afraid of everything.

Demon faith is as catastrophic to the church as atheism. It believes God exists, but doesn't believe He works. The twelve spies believed God's command enough to go ahead and check out the promised land. But due to demon-caliber faith, they didn't believe God could keep His vow. Fear will always short-sheet your faith.

Demon faith gives heed to most of God's commands, but ignores His promises. Obedience is pushed while acceptance is neutralized.

Christian faith insists that we ignore human

threat—as visible as it may be. "For God has not given us a spirit of timidity, but of power and love and discipline" (2 Tim. 1:7). Faith is fearless. Faith doesn't just acknowledge the entity of God. It trusts Him to take action even when it seems impossible.

The second chapter of James does not emphasize the importance of a Christian working as much as it promotes doing Christian work; believing. The text calls for faith to go to work. Faith is not a word. It is a movement.

James points out the futility of merely speaking words of comfort to a person in need, without offering true assistance. And, how does the next verse read (2:17)? Does it say, "Even so a Christian, if he has no works, is dead, being by himself?" Or, does it declare, "Even so faith, if it has no works, is dead, being by itself."

Our responsibility in obedience to His will is to display a faith that works. What good is a faith dressed up in Bible-class words with no place to go? Sadly, far too much faith is discussed in our church buildings, then spends the week unemployed. It cannot find decent work.

Does James 2:20 read, "A Christian without works is useless" or, "Faith without works is useless"? And how does verse 22 read? "You see that a Christian was working and the result is that by works a Christian is perfected"? No. Rather, "You see that faith was working with his works, and as a result of the works, faith was perfected." A Christian without works is dead or faith without works is dead (v. 26)?

Demon-faith keeps one's belief system on the

proverbial "round-tuit" format. Always planning to trust God, but due to fear, one never gets a round-tuit. Real faith is trusting that God will do what is needed for the moments' "daily bread."

Do note that, of course, the believer is deeply involved in working faith (James 2:14–26). Having an understanding of a working faith versus the working Christian does not imply that the Christian does not function. He must function. He is to work while holding a conviction that is not held hostage by fear. He is to work with the assurance that God works, that He will be there, that He provides.

The writings of James do point out that the person is justified when his faith is laboring. Faith is not justified; a person is. Abraham released his faith and God delivered. Abraham took action because his faith was well oiled and in good running condition. (Abraham himself was not in good running condition. The truth is he was old—too old.) Abraham knew that he, personally, was unable. However, he was sure God could execute whatever was necessary.

Mother is making toast for Laura. She places the bread in the toaster. Sixty seconds later "pop" and the crusted bread rises. Did mother make the toast? No. She made moves because faith assured her that this electric unit would warm the slice. Because she was convicted that the kitchen appliance was productive, she moved without restraint.

Faith turns the needed work over to God for His production. He can do it. He is able. As the mother did with the bread, release the matter that is in your hands and let Him complete the work.

Faith Provides Confidence

"And such confidence we have through Christ toward God. Not that we are adequate in ourselves to consider anything as coming from ourselves, but our adequacy is from God" (2 Cor. 3:4,5). Nothing is produced by our own ambition. All that we accomplish is because we are certain of God's provision. We believe He is able, through us.

Faith allows soldiers of Christ to be at ease. Work needs to be done. Lives need to be changed. Poor ones must find help. Mourners must be comforted. Faith makes one neither lazy nor indifferent. Rather, it lets God have the room in His shop to prepare and repair without our restraining bossmanship.

I have learned to be content in whatever circumstances I am. I know how to get along with humble means, and I also know how to live in prosperity; in any and every circumstance I have learned the secret of being filled and going hungry, both of having abundance and suffering need (Phil. 4:11,12).

And what is this secret? Believing that He provides the power. "I can do all things through Him when he strengthens me." "And my God shall supply all your needs according to His riches in glory in Christ Jesus" (Phil. 4:13,19)

Unbelievers don't think God supplies. They lean

on fate; they believe it just happens. Sadder still, some Christians even think this way. They believe only what they can see. But true faith is the assurance of things hoped for, the conviction of things not seen.

God is not unemployed. His divine work is based on the release of human, working faith. Jesus bestowed healing and forgiveness on those who possessed, not great intentions or accomplishments, but faith.

Finally, this segment of the book will conclude by calling us to a disposition of faithfulness. Refrain from being frantic and in a panic. Don't roll up your sleeves of human determination in the name of faith. Rather, roll up your sleeves of faith in a determined God.

Let go of bossing, complaining, whining, biting, devouring, and judging. Trust God to do much with your faith. When Jesus completed His three-year internship on earth, He had converted no one. His own disciples still didn't understand him.

So when you see someone else not living at the level you think they should, back off. Don't bristle with that squint-eyed look of contempt. Rather, show your faith. God trusted you when you were unworthy. Faith in Him says we can trust Him with others.

If it is to be, it is up to Him. We are servants, not Master. We are followers, not Lord. We are saved, not Savior. We are injured, not Counselor. We are graced, not God. We are creatures, not Creator.

In the story of the prodigal, the sinful brother

had nothing but trust in the Father. The elder brother, on the other hand, was good in his own sight. He was angry at his kid brother and plenty perturbed with his father. The guy did not have a disposition of faith. He had the facts based on what he saw, and he was hopping mad.

Be of faith. Be of God. The disposition of faith will give us room to breathe. We could all use this fresh air.

God calls His followers to be courageous, fearless, and confident. He will neither abandon nor forsake us. Don't live another hour in the crazed mentality of fear. Cities and nations are bankrupt—hopelessly squandering their present moments, trying to stay afloat. Good people plead for relief. Faith in the marvelous, provisionary Lord will bring the gentle hand of hope to these lands.

Chapter 9

How to Unleash Faith

And after He had come into the house, the blind men came up to Him, and Jesus said to them, "Do you believe that I am able to do this?" They said to Him, "Yes, Lord." Then he touched their eyes, saying, "Be it done to you according to your faith" (Matt. 9:28,29).

Again, "I pray that the eyes of your heart may be enlightened, so that you may know what is the hope of His calling, what are the riches of the glory of His inheritance in the saints and what is the surpassing greatness of His power toward us who believe" (Eph. 3:18,19).

Realize Available Inventory

Knowing that the word calls us to unleash personal faith helps us feel secure as we begin. God wants us to know of the hope, resources, and power that are available to believers. Furthermore, He goes out of His way to avoid placing any hint of burden on our shoulders.

"These are in accordance with the *working* of the strength of His might" (italics added—Eph. 3:19). Focus on the resources available to those who believe that He works. Don't be afraid.

Realize That Faith Governs God

How many men spied out the promised land? Twelve. How many believed it wouldn't work? Ten. How many believed God? Two. How many eventually entered the desired territory? Two. Which two? The two that believed God.

God provides for those who believe and not for those who won't. Fear and disbelief unplug the power supply. God simply wants us to believe Him.

Take care, brethren, lest there should be in any one of you an evil, unbelieving heart, in falling away from the living God. . . . for who provoked Him when they had heard? Indeed, did not all those who came out of Egypt led by Moses? And with whom was He angry for forty years? Was it not with those who sinned, whose bodies fell in the wilderness?

And to whom did He swear that they should not enter His rest, but to those who were disobedient? And so we see that they were not able to enter because of unbelief (Heb. 3:12,16–19).

A lack of faith is disobedience.

"Therefore, let us fear lest, while a promise remains of entering His rest, any one of you should seem to have come short of it. For indeed we have had good news preached to us, just as they also; but the word they heard did not profit them, because it was not united by faith in those who heard" (Heb. 4:1,2).

According to this, we should not fear that God works. Rather, this word says that we should be afraid when we conclude that He doesn't. God waits for us with lavish provisions that He distributes on the basis of our faith.

To repeat, we should not hesitate to unleash a dynamic, expectant faith for fear that the absurd or radical will follow. The opposite is true. We should be alarmed at the thought that we might severely limit God by forcing Him to work in our court, under our advice, by our control.

Refuse to Let Known Failures Rule

Whether the topic is prayer, giving, suffering, or evangelism, any faith effort may be matched in conversation by a story of failure. Such deflates hearts that contain momentum. More than likely, hundreds of wonderful and amazing efforts have been aborted due to the negative talk of an unbeliever. And, by the way, what is his trump card? That mighty tool of fear.

Failure should not cause us to conclude that God will not work in that area. The disciples failed, but Jesus did not quit discipling. The church has messed up, but God has not abandoned the church. We have studied the Bible with people, only to have them reject the good news; but this doesn't keep us from approaching more students.

Giving has been abused. This doesn't negate God's call for us to give liberally. Sometimes it seems that our prayers go unanswered. Yet, to avoid prayer is a terrible mistake. Don't fail to express faith in prayer simply because someone prayed for an ill person and that person didn't recover.

The people of Jesus' hometown took offense at His wisdom and power. He did not do many miracles there because of their unbelief. However, Jesus did not conclude that his powers were gone. Rather, he pursued a receptive territory.

Regardless of the bad news, faith keeps seeking the work of God.

Raise Your Expectancy Level

Dallas Willard says it well:

I want us to take the disciplines that seriously. I want to inspire Christianity today to remove the disciplines from the category of historical curiosities and place them at the center of the new life in Christ. Only when we do, can Christ's community take its stand at the present point of history. Our local assemblies must become academies of life as it was meant to be. From such places there can go forth a people equipped in character and power to judge or guide the earth.

Multitudes are now turning to Christ in all parts of the world. How unbearably tragic it would be, though, if millions of Asia, South

America and Africa were led to believe that
the best we can hope for from the Way of
Christ is the level of Christianity visible in
Europe and America today, a level that has
left us tottering on the edge of world destruction. The world can no longer be left to mere
diplomats, politicians, and business leaders.
They have done the best they could, no doubt.
But this is an age for spiritual heroes—a time
for men and women to be heroic in faith and
in spiritual character and power. The greatest
danger to the Christian church today is that
of pitching its message too low.[12]

I believe we presently practice only a fragment
of a particle of mustard-seed faith. It doesn't take
much (only a mustard seed's-worth) to get a lot
accomplished. The days ahead seem to be aimed
at revealing to mankind a word to strengthen and
expand faith. I believe we are going to be led into
greater prayer, unfathomable results, and magnif-
icent walks with the Spirit of God.

Faith's expectancy level will increase through
prayer. We will pray more. We will become aware
of His resources as we pray. It is happening now.
Paul Cho says:

Not only in our church, but in most churches
in Korea, our prayer time begins at 5:00 A.M.
We regularly pray for one or two hours. After
our prayer time, we begin normal routines
of our day. Since the most important thing

in our lives is prayer, we have learned to retire early. On Fridays, we spend the entire night in prayer. Many of our visitors are surprised to see our church packed with people for our all-night prayer meeting.[13]

I have had pastors and evangelists ask me how they can experience the same growth in their church as we are accustomed to in Korea. Yet, after meetings, they go out to eat and can spend many hours in fellowship. In the morning, they are too tired to pray. Having experienced this all over the world over many years, I decided to write this book. I hope that men and women of God will get serious enough about revival to get serious about their prayer life.[14]

Revival is in the wings and is packaged for delivery. Expectant faith via prayer will initiate the movement.

No longer will we seek church survival or even church growth. Leaders should be preparing for revival, because people are going to express the belief that God works.

Burkhardt writes: "I fear for the lawyer whose only life is corporate tax, the doctor whose whole existence is someone else's prostate, the business executive whose single responsibility is to his stockholders, the athlete who puts all his eggs in an 18 inch basket, the theologian who thinks the world can be saved by theology. . . . A closed mind

kills marriages and human relations; it deadens
feelings and sensitivities; it makes for a church
that lives in a thousand and one tunnels, with
no communication and no exit."[15]

Our minds are now curious enough to let the
windows of heaven open so that we might receive
the glorious partnership of God.

Oswald Chambers says, "Abraham surrendered
himself entirely to the supernatural God. Have
you got hold of a supernatural God? Not, do you
know what God is going to do? You cannot know,
but you have faith in Him, and therefore He can
do what He likes. Has God been trying to bring
into your life the fact that He is supernatural,
and have you been asking Him what He is going
to do? He will never tell you. God does not tell
us what He is going to do; He reveals to us who
He is. (See John 14:12–13.) Do you believe in a
miracle-working God, and will you go out in surrender to Him? Have you faith in your holiness
or in God? Faith in your obedience or in God?
Have you gone out in surrender to God until you
would not be a bit surprised at anything He did?
No one is surprised over what God does when once
he has faith in Him. Have you a supernatural
God or do you tie Him up by the laws of your
own minds?"[16]

If we ever tap the full intention and dimension
of faith, some will still try to restrict it to the
era of the apostles. Faith in the working, active, living God will generate outrageous productivity.

Convert to Grace

Grace is God flowing in. To block grace is to
block God. To trust in ourselves is to live in painful
awareness of personal inadequacy. Our next stage
will be fear . . . fear of failure, fear of misguidance,
and fear of God.

Brennan Manning wrote, "We need a new kind
of relationship with the Father that drives out
fear and mistrust and anxiety and guilt, that permits us to be hopeful and joyous, trusting, and
compassionate. We have to be converted from the
bad news to the good news, from expecting nothing
to expecting something. The right time has come,
Jesus said, 'and the Kingdom of God is near. Turn
away from your sins and believe the Good News'
(Mark 1:15). Turn away from the sins of skepticism
and despair, mistrust and cynicism, complaining
and worry."[17]

A very religious man was thankful he hadn't
neglected the will of God (Luke 18:9–14). He did
a lot right and avoided a lot wrong. However, he
trusted in himself and viewed others with contempt. This man represents much of religion now.
The lack of grace leaves disciples duty-bound, irritable, and merely self-productive.

Convert to grace.

"And God is able to make all grace abound to
you, that always having all sufficiency in everything, you may have an abundance for every good
deed" (2 Cor. 9:8). Do grace-oriented people work?
Yes, and they have abundance for every good deed.

For by grace you have been saved through
faith; and that not of yourselves, it is the gift
of God; not as a result of works, that no one
should boast. For we are His workmanship,
created in Christ Jesus for good works, which
God prepared beforehand, that we should walk
in them" (Eph. 2:8–10).

Grace is known by faith. We view the working
of God that we might be involved in good works.
Convert to grace and work will be proper and fruitful. Remain in self-effort, and not only will efforts
fail, but disgust toward others will escalate.

Start Walking

G.K. Chesterton said, "Christianity has not so
much been tried and found wanting, as it has been
found difficult and left untried." How, then, do
we try? How do we approach the call of God with
a newly resolved faith? Where do we start?

Begin in prayer. Finish in prayer. In between
the two? Pray.

Jesus was baptized. He faced the monumental
task of identifying with the human race, training
twelve good men, and bringing salvation to a mas-
sive world—a world that spanned every decade
of every century of every nation. Where did he
begin? He took forty days off to fast and pray.
Because of the significance of the work Jesus had
to do up to, during, and beyond the cross, it was
crucial that he enter into sync with God before
he entered the marketplace for us.

Once the disciples pretty well had the wrinkles of confusion ironed out after his resurrection and appearing, they were ready to go. Their first command (Acts 1:4) was not to leave Jerusalem but to wait. Before any of us go . . . once we've determined to finally accept such responsibility . . . our first move is not to move but to wait in prayer.

Don't force your way into a ministry. Wait on God to open the way.

We gathered for prayer in one of our 6:00 to 7:00 A.M. sessions. Among many other things, we prayed for Spanish opportunity. That's all. No plan, no idea . . . just seeking God's work. A few weeks later a stranger, Jose Lozano, approached us about beginning a Spanish work in Tulsa. We did not have the funds, but we had the Father. Jose and his family are serving alongside us today, sowing seed in the Spanish community, building a church.

Waiting in prayer is the basis for launching faith. Carnal eagerness and fleshly enthusiasm are merely church fireworks. The display will be seen only for a moment and by morning will be completely forgotten. "Yet those who wait for the Lord will gain new strength" (Isa. 40:31). The church where I serve approaches waiting in prayer from many angles. I share these with you.

Week-long chain prayers. A list of ten needs are given to the members. Then we all sign a sheet several times to fill in all the 30-minute prayer opportunities.

Sample

Ten items for prayer

1. Our assemblies	6. The ill
2. Our hearts	7. World needs
3. Our missionaries	8. Opportunities
4. His presence	9. Jane Doe
5. His praise	10. Our ministers

Sign up Sheet

Sunday	Midnight–12:30 A.M.	Tom Haimes
Monday	12:30– 1:00 A.M.	Missy Jones
	1:00– 1:30 A.M.	Edith Smith
	*	
	*	
	*	(Complete from
	*	Sunday Midnight
	*	through the next
	*	Sunday 6:00 A.M.)
	*	
	*	
Friday	2:30– 3:00 P.M.	Bill Edwards
	3:00– 3:30 P.M.	Missy Jones

Using this method, God hears from us the entire week. Even grade schoolers participate. As one sets his alarm for 3:00 A.M. to arise, pray, and finish at 3:30, another across town will arise at 3:30 A.M. to pick up the prayer baton.

Seven groups to pray and fast. Every May we divide into seven groups. Each group commits to fast and pray on a given day of every week. Group one will participate every Monday in May. Group two will pick up the baton with prayer and fasting each Tuesday of that month, etc. until each day is claimed.

Week-long morning assemblies. One other method is to have an assembly each morning for a week from 6:00 to 7:00 A.M. It is meaningful to divide the gathering into groups of three, four, or five and scatter throughout the room with all groups praying simultaneously.

Saturday-morning assemblies. Every Saturday, a group assembles to meet with God from 7:00 to 8:00 A.M. A prayer-request box is kept in the foyer to collect requests for this meeting.

As we start walking by faith, we need to be reminded that we are not afraid to expect God to work. We believe He does. Believing He does, once we have entered into communion with Him, opportunities for service, expansion, and growth will parade by. We will find not only the wisdom, but the strength, to approach the opening. Finally, being connected to the vine, we will bear much fruit (John 15:4,5).

Afraid God works? Afraid He doesn't?

> *There is no fear in love; but perfect love casts out fear. . . . For whatever is born of God overcomes the world; and this is victory that has overcome the world—our faith* (John 4:18, 5:4).

Chapter 10

Where Do We Go from Prayer?

Stay with Jesus. Watch him move about, ponder, act, and relate. He is right. He alone is grace and truth, peace and passion. Abandon selfishness and prejudice. Give him permission to redirect you at a moment's notice. Avoid bias. Let tradition be that of Jesus and not of the church. Our partisan minds have impaired our sweet communion with the Spirit of Christ. Remain in the body, love the brotherhood . . . but follow only Jesus.

Let Him Lead Us Out of Ourselves

Pride is a dirty five-letter word. Its mission is to keep us centered inwardly. Self-centered. It matters not whether self-attention is spent boasting of profound success or bemoaning disarming failure. It is clear: God opposes the proud.

Cho wrote in *The Fourth Dimension II*, "I discovered that one can take refuge in self-doubt and self-pity. Pride will keep a person with inferiority complexes from breaking out of his personal problems and beginning to dream great things. Once

I fell in love with the Lord Jesus Christ, and His Holy Spirit started directing the love of God towards His people, I could no longer hide within myself. I had to step out in faith and believe God for greater things."[18]

And Oswald Chambers reiterates the thought, "Self-pity is taking the wrong standpoint, and if self-pity is indulged in, before long we will take part in the decaying thing instead of in that which grows more and more into the glory of God's presence."[19]

God has called us out of darkness into His marvelous light (1 Peter 2:9). Let us pull away from thinking that defends barriers of pride. Let us not own a gospel of man's mentality, but one of the ascended Christ.

Let Him Lead Us Into the Valleys

Mountaintop days are great. Everyone loves to be on top of the world. But we must remember that Jesus left his heavenly estate to hold our hands and rub down our sore necks, down where we live . . . in the valley (Phil. 2:6,7). Faith is so appealing . . . on the high road. However, the low road is where we often reside. Faith is perfect for valley days. Listen to what Chambers has to say.

The test of spiritual life is the power to descend; if we have power to rise only, there is something wrong. We all have had times on the mount when we have seen things from

God's standpoint and we wanted to stay there;
but if we are disciples of Jesus Christ, He
will never allow us to stay there. Spiritual
selfishness makes us want to stay on the
mount. We feel so good, as if we could do anything—talk like angels and live like angels,
if only we could stay there. But there must
be the power to descend; the mountain is not
the place for us to live, we were built for the
valleys. This is one of the hardest things to
learn because spiritual selfishness always
wants repeated moments on the mount.[20]

Conflict, struggle, stress, and plain problems
should not be viewed as interference to the Christian. We are not impaired by these. Rather we
are strengthened. "All discipline for the moment
seems not to be joyful, but sorrowful; yet to those
who have been trained by it, afterwards it yields
the peaceful fruit of righteousness" (Heb. 12:11).

Everybody wants the church to grow. Few want
to work with the dead, as Ezekiel did. Everybody
wants faith to fuel them. Few want to test it out
as Abraham did with Isaac. We approach faith
the way we approach retail appliances. We are
willing to make the purchase, but we don't want
to have to assemble it, too. It's one thing for me
to surrender the cash to buy the bicycle; it is quite
another to buy it . . . in a carton . . . to be assembled at home. I don't want to bother. Also, to be
honest, I don't know how, and I don't want to
read the instruction manual to find out.

We tend to want faith to be preassembled, ready-to-go, ready-to-wear . . . but mainly ready. We view interference in our Christian walk as evil, when God uses it for good. The ugliness of the cross ought to dissuade us from satin-pillow and padded-pew religion.

We cannot press for instant faith. While living in the valley, we are actually being assembled. We go through trials to grow. Distractions are the wrenches God uses to put us together. Disappointments and struggles are the nuts and bolts that fasten the body together.

Many merely go to assemblies. They go in their carton and leave in their carton. They never risk coming out of the carton to be assembled. Whether you are on a mountain peak or a high horse, you must come down. Jesus did. "Although He was a Son, He learned obedience from the things which He suffered. And having been made perfect, He became to all those who obey Him the source of eternal salvation" (Heb. 5:8,9).

Let Him Lead Us to the Mysterious

Life is outrageously huge. The kingdom does not revolve around us because we are not the axis. Nor are our conclusions of truth the axis. Jesus is. He is far more than we. God is able to do more than we can ask or think. This is why the church began in awe (Acts 2:43). God was working. Let there remain the truth of mystery. It's legal. Be not afraid that He works.

In regard to the vast and limitless, Deepak Chopra wrote:

> A brain scientist in effect stops time to exam-
> ine a cascade's components. The chemicals he
> wants to find are extremely minute—it took
> three hundred thousand sheep brains to yield
> a single milligram of the molecule the brain
> uses to stimulate the thyroid. Nor are the cell
> receptors easy to grasp. They constantly dance
> on the surface of the cell walls and change
> their shape to receive new messages; any one
> cell may contain hundreds or even thousands
> of sites, only one or two of which can be ana-
> lyzed at a time. Science learned more about
> brain chemistry in the last fifteen years than
> it knew in all of previous history, but we are
> all still like foreigners trying to learn English
> from scraps of paper found in the street.[21]

The point? Be impressed with the boundless,
the immeasurable, the nondetectable truths of
truth. Faith: there is more to the kingdom than
meets the eye. Oh God, let us be impressed.

"We speak God's wisdom in a mystery," said
the apostle, "the hidden wisdom which God predes-
tined before the ages to our glory" (1 Cor. 2:7).
Once we lose the mysterious element of faith, we
are left with the mundane of living. We keep trying
to jump-start our faith, but after a while it just
won't hold the charge.

I love the story of Bill Edens. Max Lucado tells
of the complicated surgery performed on this fifty-

one-year-old blind man. After half a century of darkness . . . he could see. "I never would have dreamed that yellow is so . . . yellow. I don't have the words. I am amazed by yellow. But red is my favorite color. I just can't believe red."[22]

Oh that I could be this over-awed by the simple all about me.

And how shall we speak when cured of spiritual blindness? "I would never have dreamed of giving in the church. It is so . . . so encouraging. And I never dared to believe that prayer could be so surprising. But my favorite thing is knowing Jesus. I just can't believe I know Jesus."

Giving, prayer, Jesus, and any other fact without mystery is terribly burdening. Eliminate the hidden aspects of God and you become overwhelmed trying to keep your god up and going. You'll come unnerved trying to keep him out of depression. Ours is not the role of the Father. We are but the child. We love His charm, admire His intelligence, esteem His ability, and wonder at His presence. We are helplessly left to marvel at . . . how very red He made red.

"Oh the depth of the riches both of the wisdom and knowledge of God! How unsearchable are His judgments and unfathomable His ways!" (Rom. 11:33).

We tend to look for so much nonessential stuff. We probe for the clever. We seek for just one good excuse. Or, we scan the Scriptures for proof. If we could but lift our eyes to the mystery, the suspense, the unfathomable!

Where do we go from prayer? We transport in

spirit from self-preference to Jesus-mindedness. Importance is understood at the canyon and the hollow, as well as the hill and the mountain. Where do we go from prayer? We go where many are not only uncertain about going, but are unwilling to go. We move toward accepting the incomprehensible. No longer do we act only on the explainable. But, we challenge the unknown to open up wide and to vigorously bless us. No longer do we restrict anything or anyone to our personal taste, personal fear, or personal faith. We will live . . . freely live in the company of the majestic, the marvelous, and the lavish. Let our only hesitation be wondering if we have given God enough credit . . . yes even enough room to do His "I AMness."

And then, from prayer we must move into the streets—not seeking people first, but seeking the fulfillment of Christ. Jesus is our goal. God predestines us to be conformed to his image (Rom. 8:29). Shift from this target, and substantial loss is incurred. He told us that if we thought we had eternal life in knowing Bible facts rather than knowing Jesus; not only had we missed the point, we had missed the love (John 5:39–42, 17:3).

"We are here to win souls, to do good to others," says Oswald Chambers. "That is the natural outcome but it is not our aim, and this is where so many of us cease to be followers. We will follow God as long as He makes us a blessing to others, but when He does not, we will not follow. . . . We get switched off when instead of following God we follow Christian work and workers. We are much more concerned over the passion for souls than the passion for Christ."[23]

Faith cannot afford confidence in method; only in the working of God. Conviction must not be in Christian work nor the Christian worker. It has to be in Jesus. We make a genuinely simplistic kingdom difficult with our human complexities. "And such confidence we have through Christ toward God. Not that we are adequate in ourselves to consider anything as coming from ourselves, but our adequacy is from God" (2 Cor. 3:4,5).

Effectiveness in the street, along the country road, and even in the ditch is due only to our relationship with Jesus. "I am the vine, you are the branches; he who abides in Me, and I in him, he bears much fruit; for apart from Me you can do nothing" (John 15:5).

This book is written to call us out of our church buildings and into a swirling, confused community. We are compelled by His love to display interest in others. But we must not take one step without Jesus at our elbow.

It's not unusual to be deeply moved over a great need to lift another up from his or her misfortune. We must move. We are in desperate need of more and more movers. However, one of the great blemishes of mankind is workers who know God's instruction, but do not know God.

Many can do Christian work without a relationship with the Father. No one can know God, though, and refrain from serving. The former leads a busy, busy church life with a built-in contempt for others whom they regard as lazy (like Martha toward Mary). The latter communes with God and bears much fruit, gently and adequately . . . because God works . . . in them.

Where do we go from prayer? We let the God of creation and of recreation out of our Sunday School box. Whether He chooses to reign from His glorious throne or dwell within our cowardly hearts, we will let Him. If He desires to send a check in the mail to cover a specific need, we will let Him. If He provides opportunity for mission work under the most bazaar circumstance, we will let Him.

We will do our best to get over the fear of letting Him roam where we cannot explain. We will do our best to put aside the self-centered, self-serving cowardice that restricts His mighty works. We will allow Him to increase us instead of us decreasing Him. We will try to leave the bossing and the guiding and the directing and the providing . . . all up to Him.

"So then it does not depend on the man who wills or the man who runs, but on God who has mercy" (Rom. 9:16).

Let us not just believe the Bible. May we believe the wondrous God revealed in the Bible. May fear of our inadequacies subside as confidence in the "I Am" becomes certain.

Don't be afraid God works. He does, so let Him. Don't be afraid He doesn't. He does, so let him. The second verse of John Newton's legendary *Amazing Grace* heralds,

*'Twas grace that taught my heart to fear, And
grace my fears relieved.*

*How precious did that grace appear the hour
I first believed.*

Dear Lord, now is the hour . . . and we believe.

Notes

1. Dallas Willard, *The Spirit of The Disciplines,* Harper & Row 1988, p. 65.
2. Oswald Chambers, *If You Will Ask,* Discovery House 1985, p. 40.
3. Oswald Chambers, *The Love Of God,* Discovery House 1985, pp. 116–117.
4. Albert Nolan, *Jesus Before Christianity,* Orbis 1989, p. 31.
5. Ibid., p. 33.
6. Willard, op. cit., p. 175.
7. Paul Cho, *The Fourth Dimension, Vol. II,* Bridge 1983, p. 76.
8. Chambers, *If You Will Ask,* op. cit., p. 44.
9. Brennan Manning, *The Ragamuffin Gospel,* Multnomah 1990, p. 88.
10. Charles Swindoll, *The Grace Awakening,* Word 1990, p. 3.
11. Willard, op. cit., pp. 106–107.
12. Willard, op. cit., Preface xi, xii.
13. Paul Cho, *Prayer: Key to Revival,* Word 1984. pp. 14–15.
14. Ibid., p. 19.

15. Manning, op. cit., p. 63.
16. Chambers, *The Love of God,* op. cit., p. 116.
17. Manning, op. cit., pp. 75–76.
18. Cho, *The Fourth Dimension, Vol. II,* op. cit., p. 171.
19. Chambers, *The Love of God,* op. cit., p. 66.
20. Ibid., p. 43.
21. Deepak Chopra, M. D., *Quantum Healing,* Bantam 1989, p. 68.
22. Max Lucado, *God Came Near,* Multnomah 1987, p. 13.
23. Chambers, *The Love of God,* op. cit., p. 51.

Bibliography

Chambers, Oswald, *If You Will Ask,* Discovery House, 1985.

Chambers, Oswald, *The Love Of God,* Discovery House, 1985.

Chopra, Deepak, M.D., *Quantum Healing,* Bantam, 1989.

Cho, Paul, *The Fourth Dimension, Vol. II,* Bridge, 1983.

Cho, Paul, *Prayer: Key to Revival,* Word, 1984.

Lucado, Max, *God Came Near,* Multnomah, 1987.

Manning, Brennan, *The Ragamuffin Gospel,* Multnomah, 1990.

Nolan, Albert, *Jesus Before Christianity,* Orbis, 1989.

Swindoll, Charles, *The Grace Awakening,* Word, 1990.

Willard, Dallas, *The Spirit Of The Disciplines,* Harper & Row, 1988.